A JOURNALIST'S GUIDE
TO PUBLIC OPINION POLLS

A JOURNALIST'S GUIDE TO PUBLIC OPINION POLLS

Sheldon R. Gawiser and G. Evans Witt

Foreword by Walter R. Mears

PRAEGER

**Westport, Connecticut
London**

Library of Congress Cataloging-in-Publication Data

Gawiser, Sheldon R.
    A journalist's guide to public opinion polls / Sheldon R. Gawiser
and G. Evans Witt ; foreword by Walter R. Mears.
       p. cm.
    Includes bibliographical references and index.
    ISBN 0–275–94722–X (alk. paper).—ISBN 0–275–94989–3 (pbk.)
    1. Public opinion polls. I. Witt, G. Evans. II. Title.
HM261.G358 1994
303.3′ 8—dc20   94–16458   # 30398487

British Library Cataloguing in Publication Data is available.

Library of Congress Catalog Card Number: 94–16458
ISBN: 0–275–94722–X (hc); 0–275–94989–3 (pbk)

First published in 1994

Praeger Publishers, 88 Post Road West, Westport, CT 06881
An imprint of Greenwood Publishing Group, Inc.

Printed in the United States of America

The paper used in this book complies with the
Permanent Paper Standard issued by the National
Information Standards Organization (Z39.48–1984).

10 9 8 7 6 5 4 3 2 1

This book is dedicated to Amy and Lucy; Naomi, Eric and Ben. Without their help and support it would not have been possible.

CONTENTS

FOREWORD

A president concedes defeat, correctly but hurriedly, while others on his ticket are still striving to get their voters to the polls.

Another campaign, another president wins approval so overwhelming as to seem almost invincible a year in advance, inhibiting challengers—one who defies the early numbers ultimately defeats him.

In a presidential primary, the front-running candidate who wins by nine percentage points is deemed to have been damaged, and so begins a slump to defeat. Same primary, twenty years later, the lapsed front-runner loses by eight points, claims to have won a comeback and Bill Clinton begins his climb to the White House.

Those capsule stories of Clinton, Sen. Edmund S. Muskie in 1972, President George Bush in 1991, and President Jimmy Carter in 1980, have one common denominator.

In each case, reactions and results were affected by the public opinion polls, exit polling and projections the night Carter lost to Ronald Reagan in 1980; the record approval ratings Bush gained in 1991 after the Persian Gulf War; and the horse-race polls on prospects in the New Hampshire primary in 1971 and in 1992.

The lesson is that public opinion polls do not only reflect what people think about candidates, issues, problems and products. The polls also condition that thinking, by telling people what everybody else presumably thinks, by setting expectations for political candidates, and in other ways, as countless as the polls that are daily fare in modern American society.

Some polls are commissioned and conducted for precisely that purpose—to influence public opinion, not measure it. How better to popularize a viewpoint than to demonstrate that it's already the popular view? Say no, and you're the oddball.

Some poll results are selectively leaked, by political managers, for example, in hopes that by claiming strength in numbers—even suspect numbers—they can make it so. But it has to be handled with care; when the polls show towering strength, inflated expectations can tarnish even victory.

These are among the games politicians and publicists sometimes play with the polls that have become ubiquitous, most visible in election years but a fixture in marketing and public relations, in making the case for or against a cause.

Even the statistics that can shape government policy are based on the techniques of polling: unemployment rates, for example, and the consumer price index.

Figuring out what most people think by sampling what some people think is an arcane craft. The numbers are easy to grasp—somebody is ahead, somebody is behind, people think X or they believe Y, the market is ready for your new product or it isn't. The techniques behind those numbers are a complex blend of probability studies, statistics, sampling techniques that can be easily and ruinously thrown off target by a seemingly minor change and questionnaires that can be skewed by a word that hints at an expected answer.

In the age of the polls, all those sins happen, all the time. There also are sound, solid public opinion surveys that offer valuable guides to the public mood on a campaign or a cause. The challenge is in choosing the valid and scrapping the rest. Knowing how is essential for a journalist, especially a political journalist, and valuable for anyone else with an interest in public attitudes and preferences.

That is underlined by the role of the pollster in the modern White House.

Nowadays, opinion analysts not only help candidates on the way up, they also become off-staff advisers to presidents. In

Bush's last, losing campaign, his sometime poll-taker became his manager.

Every president since John F. Kennedy has had a pollster in the kitchen cabinet, or closer.

To a man, they say they never sought to affect policy, although each had an impact on strategy in office, as in the campaigns.

Stanley Greenberg, Clinton's poll man, said he considered his principal task to be keeping the president in touch with America. According to Greenberg, public opinion data aren't used to formulate positions on issues but, rather, to help Clinton in gaining support for the policies he's already set. With the decline of political parties and other organizations that once reflected that mood, Greenberg said, the public is fragmented, and sometimes alienated, and a president needs polling data for information and perspective on what people think.

Since what people think is affected by the polls about what other people think, that's power, squared.

In *A Journalist's Guide to Public Opinion Polls*, Sheldon Gawiser and Evans Witt answer questions about polling: its techniques, flaws, abuses, values, triumphs and high-profile disasters, dating from Alf Landon's imaginary lead over Franklin D. Roosevelt in 1936.

They can explain that, and do. With an understanding of that historic blunder, it is easier to understand what can go right and wrong in a modern, scientific opinion survey.

For most of us, including many of us who write about polls, the inside of a poll is a maze. Getting in is easy. This book is a guide to getting out, too, and reporting on the whole process, responsibly and readably.

Not infrequently, the word from the guides is to forget it, spike that poll because it is flawed, or at least suspect, and not worth writing about. Counterfeit polling is not uncommon; Witt and Gawiser know how to spot the phonies.

While this is a journalist's guide, the value is not limited to our line of work. Anyone who can figure out what polls mean and why, which to heed and which to dismiss, comes out ahead in this era of the pollster.

Louis Harris, a pioneer in the political polling trade, says that as polling became an increasingly important part of the campaign system, beginning in 1960, people became increasingly cynical about politics.

Harris said he hoped it wasn't cause and effect.

But there's obviously a connection.

Since candidates and elected officials, including presidents, use polling data to shape strategy, people have come to suspect that those who try to lead them often begin by following the public opinion discerned by campaign pollsters.

Politicians deny it. After all, the "profiles in courage" of John F. Kennedy's Pulitzer Prize-winning book were figures who led against the popular current, risking political rejection to do what they deemed right.

It reflects a strain as old as democracy, the question of whether a leader is elected to make decisions on principle, even when voters differ, or whether he should be guided by what the voters want. Both, probably, because losers don't get to make political decisions on either basis.

That's the kind of bedrock question that flows from the rise and influence of polls on American society. There are no textbook answers. But for the book on the how, why and reliability of all those polls, you've come to the right place.

Walter R. Mears

ACKNOWLEDGMENTS

The authors would like to thank three important groups of people for their assistance.

First, the survey researchers who have contributed so much to our knowledge and to the field. We want to thank all the members of the American Association for Public Opinion Research (AAPOR) who made us welcome as new members many years ago and who continue to welcome newcomers warmly. Also, the members, officers and trustees of the National Council on Public Polls who assisted us in our earlier work and who were supportive of this endeavor.

Most of all, we want to thank two special researchers who provided much-needed guidance early on and who clearly inspired us with their warmth, intellect and companionship. Paul Sheatsley and Herb Hyman not only showed the way but also always had time to talk. Paul always reminded us that he was a journalist before he became a pollster. And Herb wondered if that was a positive or a negative statement.

Second, we have to thank the professional journalists, both broadcast and print, who have worked with us. From the world of broadcast journalism we want particularly to thank Tom Brokaw, David Brinkley and John Chancellor. From print, Walter Mears, Lou Boccardi and Jon Wolman. Finally, Roy Wetzel and Burl Osborne, who are responsible for bringing us together in the formation of the AP/NBC News Poll in the 1970s.

Finally, we particularly want to thank those who read this manuscript, who contributed ideas and who have provided us with guidance. These include Roy Wetzel, Harry O'Neil, Burns Roper, Norman Bradburn, George Bishop, Andy Kohut, Warren Mitofsky, Mary Klette, Margaret Campbell, Kathy Frankovic, Jennifer Shattuck, the entire staff at Gawiser Associates and all of you who sent us comments on our first work.

A JOURNALIST'S GUIDE
TO PUBLIC OPINION POLLS

Chapter 1

THE OPINION TRIANGLE

INTRODUCTION

"Clinton Leads, Poll Shows," says the headline on the morning newspaper. The lead story on the network news program is the latest poll results on Americans' views on the economy. The radio headline on the hour chronicles a sharp drop in public approval of the president.

Almost every day, Americans read, see and hear reports of surveys of public opinion in the news media. It seems there are more and more polls every year, telling us what everyone is thinking on every possible topic.

Polls are not just another story in the newspaper, another item on the television news. Polls and journalism are increasingly intertwined in ways both apparent and subtle.

Today, polls are an important tool on the journalist's workbench. Many news stories focus on the results of polls on a wide variety of topics from various sources. Editors and producers often ask reporters if they have any poll results on the topic of a story, either to broaden the story's scope or to support the conclusions.

A large number of media organizations also conduct and report on their own polls. Thus, it is the journalists who are picking the topics for the surveys and who are deciding the timing of the interviews, rather than waiting for others to determine what facet of public opinion will be examined this week.

Polls measure what the public thinks. And what the public thinks on many issues is shaped, in part, by what people learn from news reports.

Figure 1.1

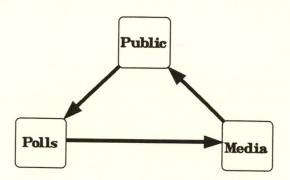

With polls increasingly a part of the news, this creates an opinion triangle connecting the public to the polls to the journalists and back to the public. This opinion triangle has become an increasingly important part of public opinion formation and journalism ever since scientific polls were first reported in the news. As this relationship between journalism and polling increases in importance, there are many issues confronting journalists.

Are polls too important? How should polls be handled day to day? Do journalists report their own polls when others would be more appropriate? Are journalists competent to evaluate polls? We will try to answer these and other questions.

HOW JOURNALISTS USE POLLS

For the working journalist, polls provide a set of tools that can be useful in a variety of ways. They can help journalists decide what stories should be done (one form of agenda-setting). Surveys can confirm or disprove information from other sources. Polls can be the basis for stand-alone stories as well as part of a larger story.

Every day, journalists across the world—editors and producers particularly—have to select which stories to pursue from a wide range of potential topics. This process (the details of which are outside the scope of this book) includes formal story conferences with reporters and field producers, daily budgets of wire service stories and informal conversations in the newsroom (see Gans, 1980). Stories that may be important to a reporter may not be of any relevance to the readers. While it is important for journalists to report on topics that the public has not considered, it is prudent for media organizations to utilize resources to cover stories that readers or viewers find significant to their lives. One of the ways to determine what stories interest people is to review the results of public opinion polls. While the editorial staff may be very concerned with the details of the latest treaty on nuclear weapons, the readers may be much more interested in crime or local unemployment.

For some journalists, the preferred method to discover what people are interested in is "man on the street" interviews. This method has serious flaws that we will discuss as we talk about the difference between polls and unscientific measures of opinion. A properly conducted poll will provide the organization with a wealth of information about what people are interested in.

The use of poll data in the news decision process is quite controversial in journalism. Some journalists consider it "pandering to the lowest common denominator" of the public's interests and an insult to the judgment of professional journalists. Others point out that journalists' shaping the news coverage to the polls is comparable to politicians' adjusting their stances to fit public opinion.

Of course there are many important issues that don't yet have the public's attention. Journalists must remember that the public's awareness of a topic is not necessarily indicative of its importance. Part of the job of the journalist is to bring important issues to the public's attention.

To ignore public opinion in the decision-making process is dangerous. After all, no one has to buy a newspaper or watch the television news. Meeting the needs of readers and viewers is the linchpin of continued public support for news coverage.

In the late 1980s and into the 1990s, David Broder of *The Washington Post* urged his colleagues across the country to listen to the voters and shape the coverage of campaigns to the voters' needs, rather than focusing on aspects of interest only to insiders. Broder's initiative called for a sophisticated use of polling data to keep the campaign coverage focused on issues that the voters think are important, rather than just today's campaign rally or the latest campaign tactic. *The Charlotte Observer* and *The Wichita Eagle* both reshaped their campaign coverage in 1992 to try to focus on the voters' interests, not the candidates' tactics.

The most visible use of polls by journalists is to base complete stories on the polls themselves.

A poll on whether or not people believe the Holocaust actually occurred provided the basis for stories in newspapers, on television and on radio across America. A poll showing a significant narrowing of Clinton's lead over Bush was the headline story on the nightly news and the next day's newspapers in 1992. The release of a survey on male sexual behavior provided the basis for stories for several days on most major media outlets.

In each of these cases, the story was the poll results and what they mean. The stories gave details on the results, put the poll in the proper context and provided technical details about how the poll was conducted.

Media organizations that conduct their own polls have the ability to plan this type of story more carefully. They may explore a series of topics over a number of polls to measure change in opinion over time or because of specific events. Knowing public opinion on race relations before and after the Rodney King incident, trials and riots can provide the basis for a well-reasoned analysis without having to depend solely upon what "opinion leaders" in the local community say.

Another major use of poll results is as a part of a larger story. Precision journalism utilizes a wide variety of scientific tools to analyze large quantities of information to improve the story. Poll results can be used in exactly that way. For example, a story about negotiations on the North American Free Trade Agreement could include information about public attitudes toward Canada and Mexico, opinions about protectionism, the benefit or threat of free trade and attitudes toward this agreement. In these stories, the poll information is not central to the story; rather, it helps to flesh out the story by reporting what the people think, without having to resort to anecdotal quotations as the only representation of public opinion.

A final use of polls by journalists is to confirm or disprove information that has been suggested by other sources. For example, during heated debates about legislation in Congress, the lawmakers' offices often report a flood of mail or telephone calls for one side or the other. They may or may not be reporting accurately what calls or mail they are receiving. (Anecdotes are often told in Washington of politicians making up the tallies of phone calls on an issue.)

But do these tallies of telephone calls mean the public is strongly on one side of the issue or the other?

Probably not.

Public officials, spokesmen for causes and others often seek to portray public opinion in ways that are favorable to their point of view. They may do this in private conversations with reporters and editors, or they may make public statements. In either case, it is important that journalists not report these personal observations of interested parties as facts; they may well be so biased that a more interesting story is how out of touch with reality these people are.

Without polls, reporters are forced to find other people with opposing points of view to express their opinion of what the public thinks. While this technique produces a more balanced story, it doesn't get any closer to what the public really thinks.

Another example of this use of polls comes in political campaigns. Representatives of each party routinely report that their candidate will win, even when they know that the chances of victory are slim to none.

How then, is a journalist to confirm the information about public opinion? The results of properly conducted public opinion polls can provide the journalist with information about what people really think.

THE IMPACT OF POLLS ON JOURNALISTS

With the continuing growth of public polls, journalists are more and more often confronted with poll results and are spending more time evaluating the polls to determine which are worth reporting.

The problem with polls for journalists is that polls are full of numbers and journalists love numbers. Numbers are solid, reliable and real. They don't have caveats or bias or hidden agendas. Or so some journalists seem to think.

"Polls had become the press's biggest bias, not liberalism or recklessness. Polls were the lens by which the press viewed everything," wrote journalist Tom Rosenstiel (Rosenstiel 1993:329).

In fact, polls have an aura of accuracy that is quite seductive for journalists. It is too easy just to report the poll numbers as truth without taking the time and trouble to see if the poll was done well and if the results are really what the sponsor says.

With the flood of polls today, the journalist has to be the gatekeeper for the public at large, sorting through the polls, throwing away the junk and reporting only the good material.

"The proliferation of polls has had a negative impact because the public has no yardstick to judge—52 percent is 52 percent," said Richard Wirthlin, Ronald Reagan's pollster for many years.

The process of sifting through the poll pile to find those bits of information that are both reliable and worth reporting requires significant training and understanding that were not traditionally part of the journalism curriculum. It is far too easy to find working journalists who have little or no understanding of how polls are conducted or of how they are evaluated.

Journalism organizations such as the American Society of Newspaper Editors (ASNE) and the Radio-Television News Directors Association (RTNDA) have conducted workshops to help educate their members. Other organizations, such as the National Council on Public Polls (NCPP), are dedicated to educating and informing journalists on the use of polls.

Leading journalism schools now teach courses in public opinion research and precision journalism. Editors, producers and reporters attend seminars and take courses to become better prepared to operate in this new environment.

For the working journalist, the greatest impact of polls is to keep public opinion measurement out of the realm of supposition and in the area of scientific measurement. Today, it is not likely that statements such as "The American public supports . . . " will get past a good editor unless poll data support the conclusion.

Political reporters can no longer sit at a local pub and report the conversation as indicative of what "the people" think. And statements by interested parties who portray public opinion as supporting their own position will seldom go unchallenged by the journalist.

The impact on the journalist is to raise the expectation that reporting will be more precise when it includes discussion of public opinion.

POLL REPORTING AND THE IMPACT ON THE PUBLIC

All of the ways polls are used by journalists shape the information that is published or broadcast in news stories. With the widespread availability of news as a formal source of information in American society today, what is reported and how it is reported have a significant impact upon public opinion.

Since polls are an increasingly important part of the world of the journalist, their impact upon the knowledge and attitudes of the public increases. Today, people can easily compare their own opinions with those of the majority of fellow residents. They can see whether the people they talk to, day in and day out, socially or at work, are typical or atypical of the population at large. Also, polls may provide a method for comparing one's own behavior with that of others.

THE SELF-FULFILLING PROPHECY

Since the information flow is from journalists to the public and back again when public opinion polls are used, some might claim that public opinion polls are a part of a self-fulfilling prophecy. And there is certainly some truth to this analysis. In some circumstances, reporting of poll results can become additional evidence as people adopt positions on issues or candidates. On an arcane topic of foreign policy, for example, it may be easier to agree with the majority of the public if one does not know much about the issue. It may also be much easier to express mainstream opinions rather than extreme opinions. Public opinion polls provide the public with information about how many others share specific opinions.

In that sense, polls can provide reinforcement of opinions that are shared by the members of the population. This is a function that has always been provided in society, first by word of mouth, and in more modern times by the media. With public opinion polls, the journalist should be reporting accurately on what the public thinks, rather than simply on his or her estimate of opinion.

Public opinion does reflect the information received by the public. As a result, in situations where free flow of information does not exist, public opinion can easily be influenced by biased reporting or propaganda. Such influences need to be considered when reporting public opinion from countries where the flow of news is controlled or restricted by the government or local customs.

In many cases, even where legitimate public opinion polls are conducted, control of information dissemination may lead to formation of public opinion that is based upon a distorted view of the world. What should be recognized by the journalist who is reporting such polling is that the poll still accurately reflects the public opinion. It is the opinion that may be biased due to the impact of information, not the poll.

PURPOSE AND USE OF THIS BOOK

This book is designed for consumers of public opinion polls. And in modern America, that is almost everyone. The intent is to provide the reader with the tools needed to understand and evaluate public opinion polls of all kinds. Whether a consumer is viewing a poll story on the evening news or poring over a press release detailing a poll, these tools are designed to help the consumer judge the value of the poll results. This book is not about how to conduct public opinion surveys; it is about analyzing those surveys.

Because journalists are one significant part of the opinion triangle, this book discusses many issues in terms of what journalists actually do with poll results.

In order to provide the greatest value to the working journalist, this book is divided into three sections. Chapters 2 through 5 discuss the history of polls and journalism and the current state of poll reporting. Chapters 6 through 13 provide the details required to evaluate polls intelligently. Chapters 14 through 18 are a guide on how to report polls, with an emphasis on political polls. Appendix A is a short course in statistics. Appendix B is a twenty question checklist written by the authors and published by the National Council on Public Polls.

Readers will benefit most by reading the book in order. Those who have little or no statistical background should read the appendix on statistics before tackling the chapters on sampling and sampling error.

If one is presented with a current problem in the reporting of polls, one can easily read the relevant chapters individually and in any order.

It is our hope that working journalists, and other consumers of public opinion, will be equipped to critically examine poll results once they have read this book.

Chapter 2

THE PRESS AND PUBLIC OPINION: ALWAYS LINKED

American journalists in the late twentieth century talk about objectivity, fairness, ethics and professionalism when they discuss their jobs. Discussions of the impact of the news media swaying public opinion tend to make journalists quite nervous.

But it has not always been so.

For much of the history of America, the press played an active, overt role in attempting to mold public opinion. The ferment that led to the American Revolution involved stirring debates in and strong stands by the newspapers of the day (Stephens 1988:185–193). In the late 1700s and early 1800s, newspapers were often openly allied with—and financially supported by—political parties and activists. It was no accident that many newspapers had names including the word "Democrat," "Republican," "Federalist," or "Independent." These newspapers printed all manner of slanders of opposing politicians. The politicians they favored always received positively glowing coverage. The negative advertising campaigns that many decry in the modern political battles pale beside the personal attacks that the partisan press launched against those on the other side of the aisle. As one paper wrote of George Washington as his second term in office drew to a close:

The man, who is the source of all the misfortunes of our country . . . is no longer possessed of power to multiply evils upon the United States. . . .[T]he name of Washington from this day ceases to give a currency to political iniquity and to legalized corruption (Stephens 1988:198–199).

As the nation developed through the 1800s, the partisan press began to change as ambitious businessmen saw they could make money in the newspaper business as well as exercise influence far beyond that of the usual manufacturing magnate. The development of steam presses allowed the printing of thousands of newspapers at a reasonable cost, helping to usher in the flourishing of the "penny press," the popular newspapers that sold for a penny each, reaching a whole new group of readers. The newspapers supported by political parties and interests waned as the newspaper business grew.

"We shall endeavor to record facts on every public and proper subject, stripped of verbiage and coloring," wrote James Gordon Bennett in the first issue of his *New York Herald* in 1835 (Stephens 1988:226).

Newspaper publishers were often men who held strong views about politics, foreign policy and domestic issues, and their newspapers reflected those views from the front page to the editorial page (although it was sometimes hard to see any difference between the two). These strong views and accompanying news coverage (which we today would call slanted news coverage) had a practical business benefit, since readers often flocked to newspapers that reflected their views so clearly. Horace Greeley (famous for "Go West, young man, go West") was an abolitionist and a man of quite strong views, many of which were obvious in his *New York Tribune.*

This trend in journalism peaked with the "yellow journalism" of the late nineteenth and early twentieth centuries, when the names Pulitzer, Hearst and others dominated the mastheads of the papers of the day. William Randolph Hearst helped push the nation into the Spanish-American War with day after day of stories in his *New York Morning Journal.*

It was a time of many newspapers across America, more than a dozen in New York alone. The competition was fierce, and many did not survive for long.

But as the nation became more and more linked by means of the telegraph, telephone and then radio, a change was coming in journalism as well.

The development of the news wire services—The Associated Press, United Press, Reuters and others—brought a different style of journalism. Starting in the middle and late 1800s, these wire services provided news stories to newspapers of all political persuasions, not just those allied with one political party or set of values. Thus, the stories from the wire services could not take sides as the news stories in some of the newspapers did. Wire service journalists focused on crafting stories without overt bias or a strong political point of view (Fenby 1986:25).

In fact, there is the view that The Associated Press (AP) created the concept of objectivity in journalism as part of its effort to define its product, its methods and itself (Gans 1980:186).

As the ranks of journalists grew larger and larger, some sought to reassess how they did their jobs and what values they brought to the task. With such luminaries as Walter Lippmann leading the way, there was increased discussion of "objectivity," of trying to rid the news stories of the prejudice of personal views and partisan politics and to "just report what happened."

Part of the reason for the change was the growing involvement of the United States in world affairs. Americans had been strongly isolationist since the founding of the country, seeking to stay out of the often violent disputes that racked Europe through the nineteenth century. Woodrow Wilson won a second term as president in 1916 in part with the slogan "He Kept Us Out of War." And then Wilson brought the United States into war, ending forever the assurance that the width of the Atlantic Ocean kept the country out of foreign conflicts.

The United States emerged from World War I as a world power, albeit a reluctant one. And newspapers and journalists had become hooked on news from outside our borders. The end of the war also brought the spread of the tabloid newspaper in a new format designed to be easy to read on the bus or the subway, with yet another burst of sensational reporting on crime, scandal and sex.

Americans turned back to domestic concerns after the war, hoping that "the war to end all wars" had put an end as well to

American entanglements with Europe and elsewhere. But it was not to be.

The worldwide economic collapse of the Great Depression demonstrated in the most painful way possible the increasing links among the developed nations. The economies of all the developed nations crashed, erasing any hope that the problems were limited to one political system or one culture.

Even as economic realities were broadening the horizons of the newspapers, a new medium was coming along that brought great changes. Radio was here.

Radio networks were the first truly national news medium, able to present the same news to everyone in the nation at once. President Franklin D. Roosevelt grasped the power and virtue of this new medium with his "fireside chats" designed to calm a nation teetering on the brink.

But with radio came a new element: government regulation. The Communications Act of 1934 thrust the government into a direct role of deciding who could own a media outlet—and what they could say. This new government regulation, coupled with the vast possibilities for profit that radio opened up, had a profoundly sobering effect on the news media. Radio news was not as partisan as that of some of the partisan newspapers, even if some of the newscasters had strong views strongly expressed.

Indeed, the news staffs of the first radio networks drew from the newspaper staffs of the era. And the newspaper staffers brought with them the increasing commitment to fairness and objectivity, as values to work with, if not reachable goals.

Chapter 3

A BRIEF HISTORY OF POLLS

ROOTS

Imagine a Stone Age group of teenagers standing around the cave one long summer evening as one asks, "Don't know. What do you want to do tonight?" While some might contend that this was the beginning of market research, others would call it the beginning of public opinion polling.

Asking questions is what public opinion polls are all about. In fact, polls are simply asking a specific type of question to a selected group of people, using a scientific basis both for selecting the people and for writing the questions.

The history of polling, therefore, must have begun when questions first were asked in a systematic way to obtain information about what other people thought. Exactly when that occurred is buried in antiquity. But more formal surveys are mentioned in ancient history. Early polls were simple counts. "Indeed, the word 'poll' comes from an old English word for head: 'pol' or 'polle.' In medieval times, the English held elections by counting heads, pols" (Weiss 1979:56). The most common such reference is to a special type of survey designed to find out who lived where and how many people there were. Such a survey is called a census.

Censuses are historically important from biblical times to the present. References can be found in the Bible, in Renaissance writings and on to today (Bradburn and Sudman 1988:15). The United States institutionalized the census in the Constitution, conducting its first census, as required, in 1790.

The U.S. census has provided not only information about people to determine the number of members per state in the U.S. House of Representatives; it has also in recent times collected more and more information about the people of the United States.

The development of modern survey research can be traced to two other important sources: market research and straw polls.

MARKET RESEARCH

Market research has been practiced informally and unscientifically throughout recent history. Reactions to samples of products were tracked to determine whether the product would sell. Product sales drove production; merchants bought what sold. With very slow communications and delivery time exceeding a year for goods from the Far East, a merchant required good instincts.

Formal market research, however, did not start in the United States until the late nineteenth century. Early projects included subjects such as agriculture and readership (Bradburn and Sudman 1988:14). The practice of market research grew during the first several decades of the twentieth century, with particular growth in measuring consumption in various industries. During this period, the first permanent interviewing staffs were hired (Bradburn and Sudman 1988:14).

The trial-and-error development of market research continued after World War I. The spread of radio brought with it all the difficulties of measuring audiences and charging for advertising. Methodology was developed and used in a wide variety of projects. The methods used were crude, although there was a recognition that samples did not have to be massive to provide useful results (Bradburn and Sudman 1988:14).

STRAW POLLS

Of more direct interest to journalists is another major contributor to modern survey research, the straw poll. Politicians and journalists have always had a vested interest in attempting to predict who would win elections. In some cases, the decision to support a candidate has been based upon an estimate of how likely the candidate is to win. (There are other reasons why support is often given to candidates who cannot win, the sacrificial lambs. They may hold other important offices or may have some truly outstanding characteristics that makes supporting them attractive.) Prior to the advent of standards of fairness in journalism, the entire news reporting of an election could be slanted on the basis of the desires of the newspaper's management.

In order to determine who would win the election, journalists have historically relied on expert opinion, typified by the party bosses or insiders. Their opinion, often not reported as such by the paper, was an integral part of the prediction process.

Such methods persist to the present day, with reporting of the prediction of party leaders and political pundits. Today, of course, these politically aware opinion leaders read the polls before they make their predictions.

The "Tom Petit" method of election prediction, named for an NBC reporter who is a great fan of it, consists of talking to patrons at a bar in the Midwest just before a national election to find out who really is going to win. We will talk about the value of such reporting later.

The straw polls, in use since 1824, most often consisted of coupons printed in the newspapers (Bradburn and Sudman 1988:13). Readers were asked to check off their choices and return the coupon. Others mailed ballots to people on various lists of names. The most famous example of this was the *Literary Digest* poll, which will be discussed in detail later.

Newspapers across the country conducted straw polls, leading to a collaborative effort from coast to coast in the 1908 and 1912 presidential elections (Bradburn and Sudman 1988:13). Large numbers of readers participated in these polls.

Another reason for straw polls was to increase readership. Even today, when this technique is known to provide virtually worthless results, publications often report that they conduct such straw polls to "keep in touch" with their readers and to give the readers "a sense of participation" in the publication.

EARLY POLLS

The most important contributions of market research to public opinion polls were development of methods and training of key pioneers.

Elmo Roper discussed the use of market research techniques in reporting the *Fortune* magazine poll. Bradburn and Sudman conclude that "Since his readers were mainly businessmen with experience and confidence in market research methods, this link was intended to increase their confidence in this new idea" (Bradburn and Sudman 1988:14).

George Gallup, Sr., began his career in advertising research at Young and Rubicam. Trained in the methods of market research, he applied them to the study of public opinion and politics. He was always involved in journalism, starting as editor of the University of Iowa's student newspaper and later teaching in the university's school of journalism.

Gallup's doctoral dissertation was based on a new method of examining newspaper readership. He was involved in testing what readers found interesting in the newspaper (Moore 1992:45).

The straw polls continued through this period, even as the scientific public opinion polls were introduced. The first Gallup Poll was published, in syndication, in 1935 and gained a great deal of attention in the press. Since the newspapers were paying for the service, the attention was not unexpected. Again, reporting of polls was considered to be a circulation booster (Bradburn and Sudman 1988:18–19).

THE 1936 ELECTION AND THE POLLS

In 1936, the stage was set for the first major confrontation between the old straw polls and the new scientific surveys. In 1936, the *Literary Digest* poll, the best known of the straw polls, mailed out 10 million ballots to households with telephone numbers, drawn from telephone directories, and automobile owners, drawn from state registration lists.

One must remember what 1936 looked like in terms of demographic characteristics of those who had telephones and those with cars. Unlike the current distribution of telephones, typically 95 percent or more in each state, few people other than the well-to-do had a phone in 1936—only 33 percent had one. While not as dramatic, automobile ownership had a similar pattern.

In addition, 1936 was a year when economic status made a great deal of difference in voting behavior. Those who were doing well were disposed to vote for Alf Landon, the Republican candidate. Those who had suffered the burden of the Great Depression were much more likely to vote for Franklin D. Roosevelt.

More than 2 million ballots were received by the *Digest*, a huge number. But that means less than 30 percent of those who were sent one bothered to fill the ballot out and return it. We will discuss later the danger of this lack of response.

At the same time that three public opinion polls—by Crossley, Gallup and Roper—picked Roosevelt by a wide margin, the *Literary Digest* predicted that Landon would win with 57 percent of the vote.

Prior to the election, Gallup predicted that the *Literary Digest* poll would be wrong and what the magazine's results would be. That angered the *Literary Digest*, but Gallup's prediction of its results turned out to be correct. Even more important, all three of the public opinion surveys got the election correct, while the *Literary Digest* missed the Landon percentage by almost 19 percentage points.

This was the defining moment in the early history of public opinion polls, for it led to almost immediate recognition of the scientific survey method. It also led to the end of the *Literary Digest*, although most analysts feel that it was in serious trouble anyway (Bradburn and Sudman 1988:22).

POLLS FROM 1936 TO 1948

The profession of public opinion polling grew significantly during the next decade. Prior to World War II, the Department of Agriculture conducted numerous survey projects and tested improved sampling methods. The scholarly journal of public opinion, *Public Opinion Quarterly*, was founded in 1937. The National Opinion Research Center (NORC), now affiliated with the University of Chicago, was founded in 1941.

During World War II, survey researchers worked on projects at home and abroad for government organizations such as the Office of War Information and the Research Branch of the United States Army.

In the elections of 1940 and 1944, the polls continued to function well and accurately. However, after the 1944 election, questions were raised about the apparent Republican bias in the poll results, and congressional hearings were held (Moore 1992:66). But the polls' reputation continued to grow, and with it the attention to methods by professional survey researchers. Hadley Cantril published research in 1944 that called into question some of the methods used, particularly the impact of interviewers on results.

In 1946, a meeting of academic and commercial survey research professionals was called at Central City, Colorado, to discuss developments in the field and how to deal with the growing industry. Nineteen forty-seven saw the birth of the American Association for Public Opinion Research (AAPOR), an organization that is still active today.

THE ELECTION OF 1948

Just as the *Literary Digest* methods had worked for years without apparent problems, so did the polling methods of the 1930s. In 1948, however, reliance on the same methodology led to a serious loss of confidence in the polls and in polling.

The 1948 election campaign opened with a serious split in the Democratic Party, with Harry S Truman as the incumbent seeking reelection, a strong Republican nominee in Thomas E. Dewey and independent campaigns by Strom Thurmond and Henry Wallace.

Early in the campaign, Dewey held a significant lead. While Truman campaigned hard, he seemed unable to overcome Dewey's early lead in the polls.

In addition, many of the pollsters based their analysis of changes in voters' opinions on a study of "Erie County (Ohio) . . . in which a panel of voters had been interviewed during the presidential campaign" (Sheatsley and Mitofsky 1992:121). In this study, done in 1940, voters made up their minds very early. Nineteen forty-eight was different.

All the national polls, including Roper, Gallup and Crossley, showed a victory for Dewey over President Truman. While the margins were not great in the Crossley and Gallup polls, about 5 percent for Dewey, the Roper survey showed a fifteen-point lead. Roper stopped polling in September, and none of the polls continued until Election Day.

In fact, Truman won by more than 5 percent of the popular vote. One of the most famous photographs in American political history is Harry Truman holding up the front page of *The Chicago Tribune* with the headline reporting a Dewey victory. The press was so convinced that the polls were right that *U.S. News and World Report* published an edition analyzing the Dewey win, Drew Pearson's column analyzed the new Dewey White House staff and the Alsop brothers wrote about the problems of a lame-duck Truman administration (Moore 1992:70).

This failure of the polls was humiliating for the pollsters and for the newspapers, who were the chief sponsors and outlets for the polls. Journalists turned quite critical of the pollsters.

The failure of the polls led some people to conclude that the methodology was just as flawed as that used by the *Literary Digest*, which had accurately predicted elections prior to 1936.

In contrast to 1936, the pollsters in 1948 were much more interested in finding out what went wrong and how it could be fixed than in trying to dodge the responsibility. They cooperated in detailed studies of the methodology that turned out to be flawed.The key pollsters, Crossley, Gallup and Roper, appeared at the 1949 AAPOR conference and discussed the problems in an open forum. Even with the mistake on the presidential race, according to a survey by NORC conducted in November 1948, a majority of the public thought the polls correctly predicted elections most of the time (Sheatsley and Mitofsky 1992: 123).

The Social Science Research Council (SSRC) published an analysis of the problems with the polls of 1948. It concluded that there was some evidence that the polls did not have a proper sample and included too many likely Republican voters from higher income groups. The pollsters were unable to accurately determine which of the voters were likely to turn out and vote, the study judged. The SSRC also found that the pollsters stopped interviewing too long before the election, missing the late trend toward Truman among the voters. The pollsters did not deal with the undecided voters in a scientific fashion, the study said.

These criticisms brought major changes in the operations of the nation's pollsters. They improved their sampling techniques, worked hard to improve the identification of likely voters and developed methods for allocating undecided voters.

In addition, the pollsters learned an important lesson about the timing of polls. Each poll is good only for the time it is taken. For that reason, polls since 1948 have been conducted virtually up until the voting begins, and some, called exit polls, are conducted on Election Day.

CHANGES IN POLLS SINCE 1948

As a result of the 1948 debacle, major changes were made in polling methodology and the polls continued to predict elections. Over a period of time, political pollsters first resisted the use of more scientific sampling methods and then finally adopted them. There continued to be controversy over the proper use of polls. Some believed that polls should not be used to "predict" elections. Others were more concerned with complete misuse of polls.

The major changes in polling over the last forty years are the result of the widespread availability of new technology: the telephone and the computer.

TELEPHONE POLLS

While it is clear that part of the problem with the *Literary Digest* sample in 1936 was the use of telephone households, today the picture is very different. Most households in the United States, more than 95 percent, have a telephone. Therefore, it is possible to provide an accurate picture of most of the population using the telephone to collect information.

This has two important advantages for polls: cost and speed. While some organizations manage to keep a staff of interviewers scattered across the country in selected sample areas, this is a very expensive method of interviewing. It is also difficult to compete in personal interviewing, since you would need to recruit a national staff or use an existing interviewing service.

On the telephone, any group of interviewers can cover the entire country and at a much reduced cost. In addition, it is possible to supervise the interviewers in one location. With the advent of competition in long-distance service and WATS lines, telephone interviewing has an overwhelming cost advantage over personal interviews.

In addition, telephone interviews can be conducted much more rapidly than in-person interviews because the questionnaires can be distributed to the interviewers immediately, and the interviews conducted one after another without any travel time between.

The results are also available for analysis immediately after the interview, significantly reducing the time needed to complete a survey.

COMPUTERS FOR ANALYSIS

With the advent of first the minicomputer and then the personal computer, the use of computers in survey research soared. Today, any poll can be analyzed on a desktop computer and most can be analyzed on a PC. The use of these systems has again reduced cost and time because the computer can be located at the survey firm and can be used to analyze the results immediately. In fact, the combination of computers and telephone interviewing produces the greatest impact on cost and timing.

COMPUTER-ASSISTED TELEPHONE INTERVIEWING

Combining computers and telephones produces CATI, Computer-Assisted Telephone Interviewing. In this methodology, the survey is conducted by interviewers who work on a computer screen. The sample telephone numbers are dialed by the computer, and the interviewer reads the questions from the screen and records the answers on the keyboard. Once the interview is completed, the information is already stored in the computer.

One of the unfortunate side effects of the technological advances has been the increased ability to conduct pseudo-polls and attempt to pass them off as real. The advent of the 1-800-number dial-in polls and the newer 1-900-number call-in polls has created serious problems. The entire issue of pseudo-polls has become an important one for journalists.

Chapter 4

THE EMERGENCE OF PRECISION JOURNALISM

The close relationship between the news media and public opinion research that characterized the first thirty years of public polling in America was torn apart in the 1960s and 1970s, as change rippled through the news business, polling and technology. The structures and channels of communication that had provided public polls to Americans since the 1930s gradually disappeared, to be replaced by a new set of arrangements and methods.

This change was driven initially by the explosive growth of television news, with its immediacy, its insatiable demand for information and its enormous financial resources. More changes came as new technologies provided powerful tools to do the polling task faster and at lower and lower costs.

From the 1930s until the 1960s and the early 1970s, there was a clear demarcation: the pollsters conducted the surveys and the news media published stories based on the poll results.

The Gallup Poll provided material for a newspaper column that was syndicated to hundreds of newspapers across the country, giving Gallup valuable publicity and newspapers a new and unique feature. Newspapers were also the main channels for Roper Reports and the Harris Poll releases.

Some newspapers, such as *The Chicago Tribune* and *The New York Daily News*, did their own straw polls, which were not scientific surveys. But, for the most part, newspapers were not commissioning polls or conducting polls for publication.

That was to change, but the change came first at the growing television networks.

In the 1950s, the television network news shows were only fifteen minutes a night. Election Night broadcasts were showcases for the network news division's talent and skills, but the tools to make the election broadcasts compelling were not at hand.

In the 1960 presidential election, CBS News used an IBM computer in an attempt to call the winner ahead of its competitors, relying strictly on raw vote totals. The race was not only to call the winner but also to display the largest vote totals on the air during Election Night.

The competition took another step forward in 1963, when the nightly television newscasts expanded from fifteen minutes to thirty minutes each evening, bringing a major expansion of news staffs—as well as of news division revenues and costs.

In 1964, the competition between the networks reached a crescendo in the California primary. In the race to get the biggest vote totals the fastest, all three networks (ABC, CBS, NBC) sought to hire stringers for each of the nearly 30,000 precincts in the state, to call in the vote totals as quickly as possible after the count was complete in the precinct. The absurdity of the situation was heightened by the fact that the two major wire services, The Associated Press and United Press International, were also tallying votes in California, meaning the nation's news media were counting the votes five times in that one primary.

Shortly after that election, the three networks and two wire services agreed to establish a pool, called the News Election Service, to count the vote for president and other top races. The competition over vote counts was over (Lavrakas and Holley 1991:62–65).

But the competition to call the races quickly was just heating up.

CBS and NBC had computerized key precinct models to try to call races in 1964, but it became apparent that just announcing the winner was not enough. The television anchors needed to talk about why the candidate won and who voted for him.

With that came the creation of the exit poll. There is some historical dispute about who did the first exit poll. It is clear that the creation of the election survey unit at CBS, headed by Warren

Mitofsky, led to much of the early work in this field. Mitofsky's group conducted an exit poll in the Kentucky governor's race in 1967, followed by exit polls in 1968 and succeeding elections. The NBC election unit was moving in the same direction, conducting exit polls beginning in the early 1970s.

THE NEWSPAPERS JOIN IN

The development of sophisticated polling expertise at the television networks was expensive. And the networks could use only a small portion of the poll material on the air. The time restraints, even of an Election Night broadcast, prevented using all the data.

The nation's newspapers were also interested in polls, as was clear from their long use of the Gallup and then Harris syndicated poll columns. The newspapers, however, wanted to be able to tie the poll stories more directly to what the editors wanted, rather than to what the polling firm desired.

In 1976, the first of the major news media polling partnerships was formed with the creation of the CBS News/*New York Times* poll. This covered not only exit polls but also extensive public opinion surveys throughout the year. The widespread use of the CBS/*Times* poll was quickly noticed, and more polling partnerships were formed.

The Associated Press linked up with NBC News, and *The Washington Post* with ABC News.

Now six of the major national news organizations were deciding when to poll, what topics to pursue and when to release the stories. The syndicated poll columns began to fade from America's newspapers.

PRECISION JOURNALISM

As these massive changes were taking place at the television networks, more subtle changes began to brew in the newspaper industry. Journalists began to look for new ways to gather data, analyze it and report it in news stories.

This search quickly latched onto the electronic computers that were increasingly available on college campuses and in the business departments of the newspapers as a potential resource.

Though the computers were still locked in clean rooms and very hard to use, journalists at last had a mechanism for handling large amounts of data in a sensible way.

In the summer of 1967, Philip Meyer applied some of the methods of social science research to coverage of the Detroit riot for *The Detroit Free Press* (Meyer 1991:ix). Everette E. Dennis took that example in 1971 when he taught a seminar at the University of Oregon and coined the term "precision journalism." Shortly thereafter, Meyer's manuscript was accepted for publication with the title *Precision Journalism*.

Through the 1970s and 1980s, the drive for more and more analysis of data in the reporting business matched up nicely with the development of minicomputers and then microcomputers that were capable of handling the data analysis task. One of the first "precision journalism" projects at The Associated Press involved analyzing the government's Current Population Survey to determine the impact of mandatory retirement practices. The AP rented time on the George Washington University mainframe computer to handle the data. By 1980, the wire service was using its own minicomputers to process its surveys of convention delegates. And by the mid-1980s, personal computers were handling the data analysis tasks.

The pattern at the AP was by no means unique, as many other news organizations struggled to distill important stories out of massive databases.

By the early 1990s, the area was increasingly called computer-assisted reporting or database journalism as it was practiced in many newsrooms across the country.

Chapter 5

THE PUBLIC OPINION POLLING ENVIRONMENT TODAY

Today, Americans are bombarded with poll results. From political campaigns to surveys on who is the best quarterback this week, we see and read about polls on a daily basis.

Poll results have become an integral part of the information flow that reaches into almost every household. In large measure, success is defined as high poll ratings.

There is a new voice of the people in American politics. It sings a continuous and beguiling tune with great range and variety. We hear it clearly but do not know what it says or what it means. Although the polls have not supplanted elections as the democratic base for a president's actions in office, at times they can supersede them. They withdraw support from winners of landslide elections, discourage some presidents from running for reelection and encourage others, and affect White House actions and the legislative agenda. Given their importance, it is surprising how cavalierly we treat them and how little we ask about what they actually mean. (Brace and Hinckley 1992:164)

THE NUMBER OF POLLS

There are literally thousands of polls done each year. Most are private, designed to assist companies and candidates in making choices and selecting strategies. Many are specifically done to influence public opinion. Others are straightforward attempts to measure what public opinion is.

One study of news media polling found 161 polls by national news media organizations in 1989, involving almost 4,000 questions (Mann and Orren 1992:20–21). In addition, the study found that 82 percent of the large-circulation newspapers and 56 percent of the television stations were doing polling of some kind. Most of it was election-related: 89 percent of the print media and 94 percent of the television stations said they did election polls in 1988–89.

This flood of polls has three important implications for the intelligent consumer.

First, because there are so many polls, it is difficult to pick out the good ones from the bad. The noise level is so high that important results of quality surveys may well be hidden. Kathy Frankovic, director of surveys at CBS News and past AAPOR president, warns repeatedly that journalists must be careful not to give equal credence to all polls. Citing such reports as the daily poll watch on the American Political Hotline (a Washington-based tip service on politics that reaches many reporters), Frankovic points out that merely listing good polls next to bad polls gives the bad polls more weight than they deserve. With the confusion, really poor poll results and results of pseudo-polls can be reported as if they were important and accurate.

Second, there are often multiple poll results on any important subject. This means that a journalist must understand how to select comparable results and to compare them. It also makes it more likely that results over time can be used to measure change in public opinion.

Third, the journalist today has a wide choice of polls, many of which do not meet the criteria for reporting. It is far different from when there were only a few polls and the results of each were considered important enough that they virtually had to be reported. In the current environment, reporting on polls can and should be much more selective, requiring knowledge and patience on the part of the journalist.

WHO IS CONDUCTING THE POLLS

With this number of polls, a wide variety of companies and organizations are conducting polls. They range from the household names mentioned earlier—Gallup, Roper and Harris—to many newer but experienced polling firms.

In addition, the news media conduct polls themselves including some of the best-known and most respected polls conducted by alliances between broadcast and print media.

Other high-quality surveys are done by less well-known, but high-quality, regional and local polling firms and by academic organizations. The two best-known academic organizations are the Institute for Social Research at the University of Michigan and the National Opinion Research Center at the University of Chicago.

A vast number of surveys are conducted by and for the federal government. Many of these are reported often, such as the surveys that produce the consumer price index and the unemployment rate. Others, with the potential for providing a great deal of information about public behavior, knowledge and attitudes are ignored by many working journalists. They can be a very fruitful source of information about specialized subjects such as health.

THE SUBJECT OF POLLS

Polls cover subjects that range from the ridiculous to the sublime. Topics have ranged from political behavior to burning of garbage; from violence in our cities to whether Gary Hart did anything wrong with Donna Rice on the yacht *Monkey Business*; from AIDS to whether the level of service at gas stations has improved.

Most public surveys today cover a multitude of topics in each poll. This provides a great deal of information for use by journalists as well as an opportunity to compare attitudes on diverse subjects. Some private surveys include questions from a variety of clients. These are often called omnibus surveys, and may cover many different topics for many sponsors. The advantage is that each sponsor needs to pay for only a part of the survey. The disadvantage is that topics may not be compatible and the sponsor cannot control the way all of the questions are presented.

A large number of polls are conducted on a single subject. These may be done for a media client, but are more likely to be sponsored by a group that has an interest in the specific topic. Advocacy groups are the most common sponsors of this type of poll. In this case, the national association of oomlaude manufacturers is likely to sponsor a poll on the quality of oomlaudes, the place oomlaudes have in the American household, and what the future of oomlaudes looks like to the public. It is likely that the sponsoring agency is much more interested in the topic than the general public and journalists. But often, interesting and surprising results can emerge from this type of survey. We will talk about the importance of looking at advocacy research carefully in Chapter 6.

WHAT QUESTIONS ARE ASKED

Not only can a poll cover a wide variety of topics, but the questions asked can also be diverse in structure and content. Questions range from simple, easy to understand and easy to answer—"How old are you?"—to multiparagraph, explanatory questions on economics or international affairs.

There are a number of standard questions about people that are traditionally included in polls. These are the demographic characteristics such as age, sex, religion, race, occupation, marital status and income. These questions are not meant for analysis alone; there are much better sources of how many people live in the East, but they are very useful in examining what kinds of people hold specific opinions.

Questions on topics of interest can range from simple yes or no answers to a wide variety of scales, options and even free response. The type of question that can be answered without restriction to a specific set of options is called an open-ended question. It allows the respondent to answer in his or her own words rather than pick from a list supplied by the interviewer. While this type of question provides better information about what is on the mind of the public, it is much more difficult to quantify for analysis.

The majority of surveys concentrate on closed-end questions. These include answer options like "approve or disapprove"; "excellent, good, only fair or poor"; "agree or disagree"; "better, worse, about the same"; "right direction, wrong track"; "better off, worse off, about the same"; "favor, oppose"; "extremely likely, somewhat likely, somewhat unlikely, extremely unlikely"; and "strongly agree, agree, neither agree or disagree, disagree, strongly disagree."

Because of the ease of analysis, this type of response is much more common. It is also much easier to report.

In addition to the type of question, a wide variety of question wording is used by different organizations. It is amazing how many different ways an apparently identical question can be asked. In many cases, the results can be markedly different, depending upon the exact wording of the question. In today's public opinion marketplace, there are many different question wordings from which to choose. Subtle difference in wording can have a profound impact on the results.

HOW POLLS ARE REPORTED TODAY

Poll reporting has come a long way since the early newspaper publication of the Gallup syndication reports. Today, most poll reports in major newspapers are written by journalists with special training, who understand the important questions to ask and the reporting requirements.

Poll stories routinely contain key information which allows the reader to evaluate the poll reported. Wire services, newspapers and network television news divisions have guidelines on the information that reporters are required to have before reporting on a poll. While not all of this information is included in every poll story, reporters must check the poll information carefully, just as they do any other source.

Many newspapers and television stations and all the networks have available to them professional survey researchers to assist in poll analysis and reporting. This allows the media outlet to produce accurate, quality reporting of poll results and to reduce the chances of misreporting.

Some poll stories include graphical representations of the results. This has provided increased reader and viewer interest in poll stories. Animated graphics are often part of a poll report on television, particularly on Election Night.

USES OF MORE GENERAL SURVEYS

Many other types of surveys are reported, not just polls. In some cases, they are not even identified as surveys. For example, the monthly unemployment numbers are generated by a survey, as are many of the economic indicator numbers reported each month.

In addition, many extensive surveys are conducted and released by governmental agencies. These can provide a great deal of useful information to the journalist who is interested in such subjects as health care, economic behavior, housing starts, manufacturing, school enrollment, crime, energy use, agriculture and spending by local and state governments.

It is very important that journalists who report these government surveys understand that the numbers come from sample surveys and are thus subject to the same types of errors as other surveys. Very small changes in indexes are sometimes given greater weight than they deserve because of this lack of understanding.

The enterprising journalist can find a wealth of background information in these sources. For example, the extensive government statistics on health care range from the experience of individuals to the distribution of facilities. Journalists make use of these statistics to find potential story topics as well as to confirm or refute positions on the provision of health care services.

Other sources of surveys of this type are academic survey organizations. These may conduct large-scale survey projects for the government, but they also conduct studies for academic purposes. These studies may provide background material or direct story ideas.

EPIDEMIOLOGICAL STUDIES

One special type of survey is the epidemiological survey. It is used primarily to determine relationships between certain population characteristics or behaviors and disease. Large-scale studies have been used to measure increased risk from smoking, eating fat, secondhand smoke and other factors. These studies can often be the key element in controversial stories such as the possible relationship between power lines and cancer.

These studies also provide interesting information about the pattern of disease. For example, certain afflictions are more common among specific ethnic or racial groups. There may also be important clues to transmission mechanisms of specific ailments found in large-scale surveys. The survey is now an important part of the arsenal of medical detectives who are trying to discover the causes of disease and disability.

AUDIENCE AND SUBSCRIBER RESEARCH

One special type of market research is likely to impact on the life of the journalist: the audience research study or the subscriber study. These studies are designed to measure the audience for media, whether broadcast or print. In addition, some concentrate on what portions of the broadcast or paper are most read, viewed, liked or disliked.

In broadcast media particularly, the on-air personalities are rated by such surveys to discover who is most popular and what characteristics of those who appear on the air are good and bad in the eyes of the beholder.

There are consultants who specialize in these types of surveys. They also provide guidance to the media outlet on how best to take advantage of the opinions of the public in order to increase the audience. While very controversial in many circumstances, these types of surveys allow the public potentially to direct the course of the media coverage.

POLITICAL POLLS

The most familiar type of private and not-so-private polling is the political poll. These are polls conducted about political situations by candidates, fund-raisers and political parties. While the majority of such polls are conducted for private use, the results are often leaked to the media when coverage fits the needs of the poll sponsor.

There are many different types of these polls. Most are designed to assist the campaign in focusing strategy. For example, it may not be worthwhile to spend any money in the southern part of the state if a candidate is sure to lose there. A poll can identify geographic areas of strengths and weaknesses. In addition, polls identify policy positions that can help and hurt a candidate. While most candidates will state that the poll had "no influence" on their position, many will admit that they will not stress unpopular positions. And quite a few political analysts think that many politicians take positions on issues only after they have looked at the poll numbers.

Internal campaign polls can help a journalist understand why the candidate, campaign, party or fund-raiser is taking specific actions. This is an important topic for those who cover politics. Candidates enter races, take positions, schedule campaign events, issue position papers, withdraw, support or attack others after review of poll results. Polls play an important, if private, role in many of these decisions. Often a journalist with good sources can determine the role that polls played.

The more obvious impact of internal political polls occurs when they become public, either deliberately or accidentally. Most often, they are released to support a specific position. These types of leaks can be extremely misleading because often the journalist cannot get the information needed to evaluate the poll correctly.

In such cases, publishing the results can be simply bad journalism, since it is impossible to confirm whether the numbers leaked accurately reflect anything.

In a famous case of this type of leaked poll, President Lyndon Johnson's staff leaked a poll of New Hampshire prior to the 1968 presidential primary. It turned out that the results were for a few selected areas of the state, not a statewide poll, which would have shown a very different result. Journalists must recognize the difficulty in reporting information that cannot be verified or evaluated.

Polls are leaked only to serve those who leak them. If a disgruntled supporter leaks a poll that is damaging to the candidate, the same rules apply. Without proper verification, the poll should not be reported.

These leaked polls can play an important part in the give-and-take of the political process. Candidates will often leak polls to demonstrate to other candidates that withdrawal is appropriate. Electability is often the subject of early polls in order to push some candidate from the race. Such maneuvering is interesting politically and is often reported. Politicians who wish to publicize such polls need to disclose the methodology of the poll so that journalists can evaluate it.

TRACKING POLLS

One special type of poll used by politicians, and more recently by the media, is the tracking poll. Basically, such a poll consists of small samples that are interviewed over a short period of time, such as one evening. Then the results from several days (typically two or three) are combined to provide a sample of opinion over that period. Each night an additional sample is interviewed, the oldest night is dropped from the survey and the results of the latest day are added. This provides a rolling average of the results from several days.

Such polls will provide a more sensitive measure of changing attitudes than weekly regular polls. With small samples, they are subject to increased error. In addition, they tend to have some potentially serious methodological problems. But they can be a very useful tool for tracking public opinion continuously over time.

Unfortunately, too often these tracking polls are reported as regular polls. This is particularly misleading if a single night is reported alone. It is also important to recognize that any change in the methods used can impact significantly on the results. Changing from three nights to two nights of polling can have an important effect.

PSEUDO-POLLS

The greatest noise in public opinion polling is generated by the nonscientific polls. That statement is an oxymoron, since a poll is by nature scientific. There are a number of names for these pseudo-polls. Perhaps the best is SLOPS, a title coined by Dr. Norman Bradburn of NORC. SLOPS stands for Self-selected Listener-Oriented Public opinion Surveys.

These polls have absolutely no value except for curiosity. They can be a lot of fun, if they are not taken seriously. A call-in poll on whether or not to cook Larry the Lobster on "Saturday Night Live," or a "poll" on who is the best quarterback on the Saturday afternoon sports program can be fun. The problem occurs when these pseudo-polls are treated as meaningful.

Too often, far too often, SLOPS are reported as polls. Local television news programs, even in major markets, conduct call-in polls by displaying a number to call for one position on an issue and another to call for the opposing position. Results are reported on the late news as if a real poll had been conducted. We will discuss the reasons why such SLOPS are of no value later. In a nutshell, the results of these attempts to measure public opinion are meaningless because there is no way to know who responded and no way to determine what kind of biases occurred because of who chose to call in.

Some journalists, editors and producers are enamored of SLOPS because they often include thousands or hundreds of thousands of participants. Unfortunately, so did the *Literary Digest* poll, and these are even worse.

FAX POLLS BY MAGAZINES AND NEWSPAPERS

One type of SLOPS that is more and more common is the fax or coupon poll by newspapers and magazines. In these cases, the publication includes a questionnaire or coupon to be returned to the publication with the answers completed.

Again, the results of SLOPS are meaningless. One never knows who didn't respond and what they think. Editors tend to defend these attempts as a way for their readers to participate in the publication. Unfortunately, that is not always the way the results are reported. For the collection of anecdotal information, they might be just fine; for measuring public opinion, they are an abject failure.

SALES PROMOTIONS

Perhaps the worst abuse of the survey process is the disguised sales promotion. In this scam, a salesperson calls and says that he is conducting a survey about some type of product. As a result of information gathered during the interview, the salesperson makes an offer to sell an item at a special price, because the respondent was so cooperative.

While this type of activity normally is not reported, this abuse has a direct impact upon polls: it makes people less likely to cooperate with reputable polling firms.

DISCLOSURE STANDARDS

During the growth of the polls over the last forty years, there have been a number of controversies about specific differences in poll results. A number of them will be discussed in the chapters that follow. These problems have produced several important results.

In 1969, the National Council on Public Polls (NCPP) was organized. Its purpose was to improve the quality of the reporting of public polls and, in order to do so, it produced a standard for the disclosure of information about the methodology of any poll that is reported publicly.

The American Association for Public Opinion Research (AAPOR) also has adopted disclosure standards for its members to use when the pollster releases results to the public.

CONCLUSION

The explosive growth in public opinion polls continues to this day. With more and more polls done, with more and more polls reported, and with more and more pseudo-polls, a journalist has an increasing problem reporting responsibly. This task requires increased knowledge and understanding of the public opinion polling process on the part of journalists.

Chapter 6

THE POLL: WHO DID IT?

It happens almost every day in newsrooms across America: while sitting at the desk, you are handed a press release trumpeting the latest poll on the environment, politics or the economy. What do you do?

As any good journalist would, you start by asking questions in order to evaluate whether you want to report this survey.

The first question is: Who did the poll?

Unless you know who did the poll, you cannot get the answers you need to all the other questions that you might ask about the survey. Very often, the press release and/or press conference will not include much of the information you need in order to decide whether the poll should be reported.

The second reason to obtain the answer to that question is that a poll done by a reputable, experienced survey research firm, an impartial media outlet or a well-known academic institution is much more likely to be reliable. This is not to say that an excellent survey cannot be produced by a brand-new firm or a local college professor. Rather, the source of the poll must be judged using the same analysis each journalist must use in judging the source of any information. You always confirm information, but you are more likely to report information that comes from a reliable source that has provided information in the past.

If the press release about the poll does not include who did the survey, and if the spokesperson for the organization that is releasing the poll will not tell you, then serious questions must be raised about the reliability of the survey and whether you should even consider reporting it.

Unless there are extremely compelling reasons otherwise, you should ignore any poll about which you cannot obtain this most basic fact.

WHY IS AN EXPERIENCED FIRM BETTER?

Recently, the medical community has reported some mortality statistics on heart bypass surgery. The results demonstrate clearly that those hospitals that perform this surgery most often, have the lowest mortality rates. Practice may not make perfect, but it often makes for better procedures and better surveys.

An experienced survey research firm is more likely to have a cadre of professional interviewers who have been well trained and are well supervised. These interviewers tend to work on many different surveys, so the poor performers are likely to be weeded out, with the better ones remaining.

An experienced survey research firm always has to worry about reputation. Bad survey work can lose clients very quickly. It is likely that such a firm is in the business for the long run, unlikely that it would provide a cheap and dirty survey for a quick buck.

A solid survey research firm maintains a staff of trained analysts who examine the results of many different surveys. They are much less likely to be committed to the results of the survey and, therefore, more likely to be objective.

These types of firms include well-known polling firms such as Gallup, Roper and Harris, as well as media polls such as CBS News/*New York Times*, NBC News/*Wall Street Journal*, ABC News/*Washington Post*, and *The Los Angeles Times*. These media polls are conducted or supervised by professional staff employed to provide survey research capability in-house. The quality of the work is similar to that of the top survey research firms.

DIFFERENCES BETWEEN PROFESSIONAL FIRMS

Even when professional survey research firms conduct similar polls, there may be differences in results caused by different techniques, sampling frames and many of the other items we will discuss below. The basic differences between firms are called "house effects." House effects are produced by differences in procedures that may appear to be insignificant but that can impact on poll results.

For example, firms differ in the hours that they survey adults, the way they select the person to be interviewed from the household, the way the telephone numbers are selected in the sample, the introduction to the survey and the way the interviewer introduces the firm conducting the poll.

In most cases, the differences between professional polling firms are a matter for academic investigation and do not produce differences that are significant to journalists.

NONPROFESSIONAL POLLS

There are a number of serious dangers with polls conducted either by advocacy groups or by others who are not professional survey researchers.

These range from ridiculous mistakes to deliberate distortion. Professional polling firms make mistakes, too, but unless these are few and far between, they are not likely to stay in business.

Perhaps the best examples of problems in using nonprofessionals come from the use of volunteers as interviewers. In a number of cases, poll results have been greatly distorted by volunteers who report respondent opinion only when it agrees with their position.

This is often true of political polls conducted by campaign volunteers. There are several immediate sources of error. First, a bias may be introduced by the respondent who is much more likely to participate in a poll by the campaign of a candidate he or she supports than in a poll for a candidate he or she opposes. Second, the volunteer interviewer, a partisan supporter of one candidate, is much more likely to interpret responses as favorable toward his or her candidate than not. Finally, volunteers may deliberately distort the results to favor their candidate.

These problems can make such surveys useless as any measure of public opinion. They are made worse because most surveys of this type do not include direct supervision and monitoring of the interviewers. There is virtually no quality control of the process.

One should always be extremely careful of any survey that has been conducted by interviewers who have a stated position on the subject of the survey.

PARTISAN PROFESSIONAL SURVEY FIRMS

Some very good professional survey firms conduct polls for only one political party. When reporting these surveys, one has to be careful to acquire all the information needed in order to evaluate the survey results.

While these firms tend to provide professional results to their clients, they may not provide journalists with any relevant information that reflects poorly on their candidate. Most often, this type of survey is conducted to further a political purpose. In that case, while the firm may well report the complete and potentially harmful results to the candidate's campaign staff, the public report of the poll may be greatly circumscribed.

Remember that the polling firm has two reasons to work with journalists: to help its client, and to build a reputation so that it can help other clients in the future. A journalist can make use of the second need to question the firm about the specific poll results.

STUDENT POLLS

Two types of polls involving students need to be mentioned here. The first is the study reported by the local university of some startling new finding about some kind of human behavior or attitude.

For example, the *American Economic Review* published a study in its December 1993 issue that said unwanted Christmas gifts add up to billions of wasted dollars in the American economy. The study said 10 to 35 percent of the value of all gifts given at Christmas is lost because of a mismatch between what people want and what they get. And that adds up to at least $4 billion in wasted gifts. What was the basis for this $4 billion figure covering all the gifts given in the United States at Christmas? Information from seventy-four Yale students in an economics class!

This study—and many, many others like it—are interesting and may even be entertaining. But they are not reliable surveys of public behavior or attitudes that have any meaning beyond a college campus. To estimate attitudes or behavior for the general public from tiny groups of college students is a meaningless exercise that should not be given credence by repetition in news stories.

The second type of poll is the survey of the population on a given topic, reported by a local college professor. It is only by asking questions about the methodology of the survey that the journalist discovers that the survey was a class project, that the interviewers were students and that they were learning about surveys and the subject matter while they were conducting the survey.

While perfectly acceptable surveys can be conducted by student interviewers under proper supervision after training, many of these class projects do not have the quality needed to provide the journalist with the level of comfort required to report the results. Even if the study appears to be well conducted and should be reported, the use of student interviewers should be mentioned in the story.

SURVEYS R US

Just because the survey firm is not famous does not mean that it doesn't do good work. Many smaller, local survey research firms produce excellent surveys, but it is more difficult for the journalist to determine their quality.

In order to determine the quality of the survey firm, the journalist should ask about membership in organizations such as the National Council on Public Polls, other industry trade groups, and the membership of key personnel in organizations such as the American Association for Public Opinion Research.

Reviewing the qualifications of key staff members is as important as reviewing the qualifications of anyone a journalist would interview directly. While survey research does not require as much training as nuclear physics, techniques and technology change rapidly, and quality researchers require training and retraining.

"This business has no entry level," said Patrick Caddell, well-known pollster to George McGovern and Jimmy Carter who has since left the field. "Anybody can announce they are a pollster and they are a pollster" (American Enterprise Institute 1993).

One key to the performance of any survey firm, local or national, small or large, is prior experience and results. It is perfectly reasonable to ask a firm what other projects it has conducted, what other clients it has served, what other public polls it has released. This not only will provide information about the experience of the firm. It will also provide clues to whether the firm conducts polls only for groups with a specific point of view and whether the firm is trying to conduct surveys outside its area of expertise.

FIRMS IN PARTNERSHIP, INTERVIEWING SERVICES

As you ask questions about a survey, you may find that the actual interviewing was done by an interviewing service rather than by the firm that designed and analyzed the survey. While this is not the method used by larger national firms, when the quality of the interviewing service is high, the results can be very good. In this case, the journalist might have to ask questions of both firms to gain confidence that the survey was conducted properly.

Interviewing services come at all levels of quality—from phone mills that fail to train or supervise interviewers to professional firms that provide very high-quality interviewers, properly trained and supervised.

THE "NIH" SYNDROME

This has nothing to do with the National Institutes of Health; rather, it refers to the practice of using only your own surveys, rejecting others as "Not Invented Here." This is very often true of media organizations that conduct their own polls. Even when another firm's poll is relevant, timely and professionally conducted, often a newspaper or television station will report only its own poll and will ignore others' efforts.

Such action is based, in part, on the level of knowledge and understanding of its own polls, but also is often affected by the desire not to publicize a competitor's poll.

The same problem exists in the major public polling firms. Most often, press releases will refer only to other surveys conducted by the same firm. But in this case, the media reporting the poll are free to utilize as many sources as desired.

CONCLUSION

If you don't know who conducted the survey, you can't get the answers you must have to many important questions in order to decide whether to report the poll. Who did the survey is an important indicator of quality, good or bad, that you need to take into account in your reporting.

Chapter 7

THE POLL: WHO SPONSORED IT?

So you know who actually conducted the poll.

Now the question is: Who paid for it? Who thought these matters were important enough to spend money for a public opinion survey?

Polls are not generally conducted for the good of the world. They are conducted for a reason: it may be to gain helpful information, to advance a particular cause or to serve a specific business purpose.

Only by knowing who paid for the poll can the journalist and the informed citizen make a reasonable judgment on the reason the poll was conducted, and thus on the poll's overall validity. The sponsorship of a poll may make very little difference to interpreting its results, or it may give you cause to disregard the poll completely.

For example, one staple of the published polls for the last two decades has been questions focused on space and the U.S. space program. The questions go into what the public thinks of the space program, should U.S. tax dollars be paying for a trip to the moon or to Mars, and the like.

Early in 1993, there was a new burst of such polls. It wasn't that there was a resurgence of interest in the space program or a new threat to make "America second in space." It was because the Clinton administration was considering killing the space station program, the last gigantic project in the space budget. And who paid for such polls?

Rockwell International, for one.

Why?

Because Rockwell is major contractor on the space station and the space shuttles that would be needed to lift all the station's materials into space.

What did the Rockwell poll show? That Americans support money for the space program.

This finding should not be a surprise, since Rockwell is a business seeking to make a profit. Trying to drum up political support on Capitol Hill for continuing a major space station effort, the company sought to show lawmakers that the voters backed continuing to spend billions on the program while the principal political debate was on cutting government spending.

It is not our purpose here to say that the Rockwell poll was flawed or that the numbers were cooked. But it is to say that Rockwell had a reason for paying for the poll and for releasing it: building support for one of its own projects. While the poll numbers may have been defensible, you can be reasonably certain of one thing: Rockwell would never have released the poll if the results had shown Americans did not want money spent on the space program.

The Rockwell polls on space—which have been conducted regularly for many years—are an example of interest-group polls. These are surveys paid for by a business, labor union, interest group, trade association, citizens' coalition or similar group. They are usually publicized through press conferences, interviews and informational handouts.

The goal of an interest-group poll is to drum up support for one side in the public policy debates that make up the messy form of government called democracy. It is designed to convince senators, representatives, bureaucrats, journalists, editors and commentators that the public really supports one side in the argument.

Interest groups from the Sierra Club to the National Rifle Association and the National Organization for Women to the American Medical Association have commissioned polls and released the results.

Some interest-group polls are quite reliable and convincing. Some are junk.

"One can make almost any point about an issue and then find a poll to prove it," says Ben Wattenberg, a political analyst at the American Enterprise Institute. "Pick your poll, pick your point" (American Enterprise Institute 1993).

Sometimes it is not that simple to determine who paid for a poll. Often the poll results are provided by a public relations firm that may not want to—or may not be allowed to—reveal the sponsor. In this case, the answer is again very simple: the poll results should be tossed in the trash can and forgotten.

Another problem that can arise is the use of foundations or think tanks as the "sponsor" for a poll. In this case, it is important to probe behind this apparent sponsorship to make certain that it is not simply a dodge to hide the true source of money for the survey. For example, a foundation may publicize a poll on attitudes toward business. If that foundation is largely supported by labor union money, it is necessary to ask if any particular union paid for this poll. In any case, the identity of the sponsor should be made as clear as possible, using such language as "the poll was paid for by a foundation largely funded by labor unions."

Not only should the reporter find out who paid for the poll, but that fact also should be mentioned prominently in the story on the poll results. For example, if a drug company paid for a poll on the public attitude toward taking medication for depression, that sponsorship should be mentioned prominently in the story. Only by highlighting this fact can the readers, viewers or listeners begin to understand the poll results.

CAMPAIGN POLLS

One special case of special-interest polls confronting the journalist comes from political campaigns.

Public opinion polls are a major strategic and tactical weapon used by the modern political campaign. They help the politicians understand what will motivate the voters, what will anger them and what will soothe them. Polls are used extensively to gauge the impact of campaign advertising and other tactics. Indeed, well-funded and -organized campaigns are now driven to some degree by the poll results.

These polls are conducted for one basic reason: to help the candidate win.

The principal goals of campaign polls are to provide feedback for the campaign managers on how well the candidate's message is being received by the voters and to provide information on which voters are more likely to become supporters if they are not already.

In the 1992 presidential campaign, the managers of Bill Clinton's effort targeted their television ads, candidate visits and money for local staff largely on the basis of polls. States that Clinton could not win—according to the polls—got no visits, no television ads and little money for staff. The states Clinton would have a hard time losing—again according to the polls—got few visits, a small allocation for ads and some money for staff. It was the battleground states where Clinton and George Bush both had a shot at winning that the Clinton campaign focused its time, attention and money.

So the campaign's own polls matter a great deal inside the candidate's own organization. But what should they mean outside, to the public at large? Much, much less.

Campaign polls have many purposes inside the campaign. One innovative technique pioneered by Patrick Caddell, and now in wide use, involves asking a question matching up the candidates early in a poll, then asking a series of questions that actually present information about the candidates to the respondents. Then the horse-race question matching up the candidates is asked again at the end of the questionnaire. With this strategy, the campaign can gain some insight into what will move voters one way or the other and what information will not sway them.

This technique, useful for the campaign, can be most misleading to the public. Various campaign aides have occasionally tried to pass off the results of the second horse-race question as the real state of the voters' views. That is misleading at best and dishonest at worst.

Campaign polls are useful tidbits of data for the political reporter. But, given the sponsorship of the poll and the reason for its existence, a campaign's poll results should be handled with great care and never published or broadcast standing alone. If at all possible, other potentially less biased polls should be used to help balance the campaign's numbers.

MEDIA POLLS

Many of the public opinion polls that are available today are sponsored by the news media themselves.

As mentioned earlier, polls are conducted and released by CBS News and *The New York Times*, ABC News and *The Washington Post* and NBC News and *The Wall Street Journal*. Other news organizations that have sponsored polls since the 1970s include The Associated Press, *The Los Angeles Times*, *The Boston Globe*, *Newsday*, *The Atlanta Journal–Constitution* and many others.

Just as with any other poll, media polls are done with a specific purpose. In this case, that purpose is to generate good news stories, flesh out other reporting and help guide the news coverage decisions inside the organization.

This motivation does not make the media polls inherently more reliable. But media-sponsored polls are far less likely to be conducted with a specific, policy-oriented point of view than polls paid for by special-interest groups. For example, a CBS News poll on the future of the space station program is not done with the intent to promote or attack the program. Its purpose is to generate a news story. Thus, one source of doubt about the poll's findings can be allayed.

ACADEMIC POLLS

Another major segment of the public opinion polls comes from the world of academia.

The General Social Survey conducted by the National Opinion Research Center in Chicago and the National Election Studies conducted by the Survey Research Center at the University of Michigan are two of the best-known polls coming from the nation's universities and colleges.

Many of these surveys are conducted principally to advance the state of knowledge about a certain area. The National Election Studies from Michigan are designed to provide a reliable, repeatable source of information on the nation's electorate.

Such studies often are sponsored by the university or the federal government, through the National Science Foundation or the Department of Health and Human Services.

Do these sources of funding make a difference? Yes, in a positive sense. These academic polls are usually done with excruciating attention to detail and fairness and are subjected to detailed scrutiny in the academic world. Such care and scrutiny should give the journalist an added sense of security in dealing with the results.

But there is a caveat here, as there often is in such cases.

Some interest groups may commission a professor or a department of a university to conduct the poll and then release the results. This is another case where the question that must be answered is: Who paid for the poll?

LEGITIMATE DIFFERENCES BECAUSE OF SPONSORSHIP

Sometimes a difference in sponsorship makes a difference in results that should be noted, though not necessarily to the point of discarding the poll's results.

Listening to political pollsters who work for Democrats and those who work for Republicans, one sometimes finds conflicts in what they are saying about the views of the Democrats or of the Republicans or of the views of the independent voters or the like. One potential source of the differences is the way some questions are asked. For example, Democratic pollsters often pose the partisanship question by asking the respondent if he or she is a Democrat, an independent or a Republican. If the answer is Democrat or Republican, then the respondent is asked if he or she is a "strong" Democrat or Republican or a "not so strong" Democrat or Republican. The self-described independents are asked if they "lean" toward the Republican or Democratic party.

This set of questions breaks the voters down into seven basic groups ranging from strong Democrats to strong Republicans.

But GOP pollsters often use a scale asking voters to place themselves on a ten-point scale where 0 is a strong Democrat, 10 is a strong Republican and 5 is an independent.

As we will discuss later, in the chapter on question wording, that is a difference that makes a difference. Results based on one of these questions can legitimately give very different results from the other question.

CONCLUSION

Just as with the question of who conducted a poll, if you cannot find out who paid for a poll, the survey should be discarded. An anonymous poll is much worse than no poll at all.

Chapter 8

THE POLL: SAMPLING

Of all the questions about polls, the one asked most often goes something like this: How can you possibly interview only 1,000 people and then claim to know what 250 million Americans think?

The precise answer to the question comes from equations, statistics and mathematics that many people have never taken the time to understand. But understanding the basics of sampling is absolutely essential to understanding public opinion polling, even if you never see an equation on paper.

If the wrong people are picked to be interviewed, the survey will be useless. If the sampling methods are not scientific, the results may be completely misleading. A properly drawn sample is a necessary condition for any survey that is not a census of the population in question.

Pollsters use various analogies drawn from everyday life when confronted by someone's basic refusal to believe in the power of sampling.

For example, if you don't believe in samples, the next time you visit your doctor, he may want to do a blood test. If so, tell him to take all your blood for the test and not just a sample.

Or when you are making soup and want to see if the seasoning is correct, don't just sip a spoonful: drink the whole pot.

HOW MANY PEOPLE WERE INTERVIEWED?

When a poll of a group is taken, a sample of the group is normally interviewed. A sample is a subgroup of the population. Any subgroup can make up a sample, but just any sample is not appropriate for a survey.

The first important piece of information about the sample for a poll is how many people were interviewed, the sample's size.

This is extremely important. If only a few people are interviewed out of a significantly large population, the results are subject to a great deal of error even if the sample was drawn correctly. For example, no matter how you choose ten people, they will not represent a very useful sample of voters in the United States. In fact, the error potential would be so large as to make the results almost meaningless. (Those who have not taken a course in statistics, which we highly recommend, should read Appendix A before completing the remainder of this chapter.)

The number of people interviewed is the most important component in the precision of the survey, measured in what is called sample error. This is covered in Chapter 11. For this discussion, the sample size on its face must be reasonable.

One of our favorite stories was written in *The Westport News* of Westport, Connecticut. The headline on the front page showed that one candidate for first selectman (rather like the mayor of the town) led the other candidate, according to the newspaper's own poll. In the continuation of the story on an inside page, buried in about the thirteenth paragraph, were the actual poll results: one candidate was favored by thirteen people, the other by twelve. Even without a statistical background, most readers, and certainly most journalists, would realize just how ridiculous such a story was.

The key is that while more is better in evaluating samples, small samples can be useful, too, depending upon the circumstances and how careful you want to be.

But there are some cases in which no sample can be adequate. For example, if a very close vote is anticipated in the U.S. Senate, only a census of the members—finding out the positions of each and every senator—would give you confidence about the results.

HOW WERE THE PEOPLE CHOSEN?

Just because you have the right number of people doesn't mean that the sample is of any value. If you interviewed 10,000 registered voters—all in the rural South—you would not learn much about national opinion. If you went to a shopping mall and interviewed everyone who came to shop, do you think they would be representative of the country's population as a whole? It is not very likely.

The way to construct a sample for a poll that should accurately reflect the population is to be rigorous about picking the sample. The rules for drawing a sample are fairly straightforward.

PROBABILITY SAMPLING

A probability sample is one in which every person in the population has a known, nonzero probability of inclusion in the sample (Sudman 1976:49). This type of sample is sometimes called a random sample. But more often than not, samples of this type are not really random at all.

A simple random sample is one in which all of the units in the population have an equal chance of inclusion in the sample and the selection of one unit does not impact on the selection of any other unit (Sudman 1976:49).

Let's look at a simple random sample. If there are 1,000 undergraduate students at a university, you can create the initial information for a sample by writing the name of each undergraduate on a separate piece of paper and putting those 1,000 slips of paper into a hat. If you then mix the slips of paper well and draw 100 of them out of the hat, you will have a simple random sample.

Let's look at why this meets the criteria. First, every student had an equal chance, one in ten, of being selected. This assumes that your list is complete, and that each student appears on it once and only once. Remember this factor, because it will become more important as we examine more complex methods of sampling.

Second, the selection of the third student on the list did not impact on any other student. We did not choose one from dormitory A and one from dormitory B; rather, each choice was independent of the others.

If you do not want to place every unit name in a hat and physically sample them, there are a number of other selection techniques that can work. The most common is to assign each of the members of the universe a sequential number from 1 to n, where n is the total number in the population. In our example above, you would number them 1 to 1,000.

The next step is to obtain a list of 100 random numbers between 1 and 1,000. This can be done by using a random number table like those included in most books on probability and statistics. Pick a starting point in the table and then take the next 100 numbers. Or it can be done by computer, using the random number functions that many computer languages include to generate 100 numbers. Whichever method is used, the sample would consist of the students with the numbers that had been randomly selected. This would be a simple random sample.

Simple random samples are extremely useful when known populations are sampled and the cost of reaching the selected units is reasonable.

Very often, there are practical difficulties with using a complete list and random number selection. If the population were 1 million, rather than the 1,000 in our example, it would take a long time to cut those pieces of paper or to number each of the names. In this case, one method to use is what is called a systematic sample.

To take a systematic sample of 100 from our list of 1,000 students, we would take every tenth name from the list. The problem is where to start. In this case, selecting a random number between one and ten is the answer. We start with the name numbered with the random number and take every tenth name thereafter. If the random number were 3, we would take names 3, 13, 23, 33, and so on.

Obviously, if the number of students was 1,006, our every-tenth-person might not produce a sample of exactly 100. In this case, there are several options available. Most often, a sample of 99 or 101 will be fine, and no change is required. In the case where the interval produces a significantly larger or smaller sample, there are two different approaches. If the interval produces too small a sample, it should be adjusted to the next interval even if it produces too large a sample. In that case, and in the case where the initial sample is too large, it is easy to reduce the sample by selecting a simple

random sample of the size needed to reduce the sample. For example, if 110 were selected and 100 desired, a simple random sample of 10 can be selected for deletion from the sample. This will not impact on the quality of the sample.

Most often, a systematic sample will produce results equivalent to a simple random sample. Only in very unusual cases will any true bias be introduced. Sudman suggests, however, that it is "important to inspect the lists before beginning in order to ensure that there are no obvious periodicities" (Sudman 1976:56). This is an important review process. If the names of students are arranged so that the first name is a freshman, the second a sophomore, the third a junior and the fourth a senior, and if this pattern repeats, then a systemic sample with an interval of a multiple of four would produce a very bad sample indeed.

Sudman reports an example of this type of problem where the last digit of the respondent number was used to indicate whether the respondent was female (an even number) or male (an odd number). A follow-up study used a systematic sample of the respondents, and the interval and starting number were both even. The sample therefore was all female and had to be discarded (Sudman 1976:56)

In most cases, however, these types of samples do not produce such a result. Remember, however, that the lists must be good and carefully checked for omissions and duplications.

WHY MOST SAMPLES ARE NOT SIMPLE AND RANDOM

Random samples are not often used because they tend to be expensive and are often not feasible. This is because they require the identification and labeling of each element in the universe prior to the sampling process (Levy and Lemeshow 1991:63). In addition, the samples produced by this method are not likely to be useful in fieldwork. For example, think about the geographic dispersion of respondents in a random sample of the population of the United States. Say you were taking a sample of 1,000 adults. Even the largest city (say, for the sake of mathematical simplicity, it has a population of 10 million people out of 250 million in the country) would have only 40 respondents. Some small states might have

only one or two respondents at most. If you were interviewing in person, you might spend a lot of time traveling from respondent to respondent. That would cost a lot of money.

With telephone number samples, a pure random sample has similar costs. Since there is no list of all working telephone numbers available, randomly generated phone numbers would be the only true random sample. Such a sample would contain mostly numbers that are not in use, and the costs to complete a telephone survey would be astronomical.

In both personal and telephone interviewing, other sampling methods are available to solve this problem.

CLUSTER SAMPLING

In order to reduce the costs of surveys, samples most often make use of the fact that the population is arranged in a nonrandom fashion. In fact, people are clustered together. In personal interviewing, the geographic dispersion of respondents is an important part of the cost. (Telephone survey samples are discussed in greater detail below.)

In a cluster sample, sets of members of the population are first selected, and then the individual units are selected from the chosen sets. Sudman points out that there are four rules for a cluster sample (Sudman 1976:70):

1. Each unit in the population must belong to one and only one cluster.
2. The number of elements in each cluster must be known or reasonably estimable.
3. The clusters must be small enough that it is cheaper to use them than to take a random sample.
4. The clusters should be chosen to reduce the increase in sampling error caused by the use of clusters.

Clusters might be counties, Standard Metropolitan Statistical Areas, census tracts or blocks or some other consistent geographic unit. For our example of college students, they might be dormitories. For nursing home residents, they might be nursing homes.

This type of sample is also known as a multistage sample. First, clusters are chosen, then within the cluster, individual units are

selected. By knowing the size of the cluster and the method of selection, the probability of the selection of any individual unit in the population is known. That means that we still have a probability sample, but no longer a random one.

There is a cost for using a clustered sample: increased chance of sampling error. Sudman provides an indicator of the loss of precision caused by the use of cluster sampling (Sudman 1976:77). For example, a cluster of size 5 (that is, each cluster has five units) increases the margin of sampling error by 9.6 percent. If the error for that sample size is 3.00 percent, it will increase to 3.29 percent. With clusters of size 10, the increase is 21.6 percent, and for clusters of size 25, the increase is 57.6 percent. So the cost reductions in using a cluster sample have to be compared with the increased sample size required to produce the same level of precision in the study.

TELEPHONE SAMPLING

Telephone surveys are possible in the United States because of the vast increase in telephone coverage. In 1963 about 20 percent of households in the United States had no telephone. This was reduced to about 7 percent by 1980 (Groves et al. 1988:29). Even with this coverage, however, there are some important differences between those who have telephones and those who do not. For example, residents of the South are more than twice as likely not to have a phone as residents elsewhere in the country. Noncoverage for African-Americans is about three times the rate for whites. And the unemployed are more than twice as likely as the employed not to have a telephone (Groves et al. 1988:29–30).

In most surveys conducted by telephone, these noncoverage issues are ignored. For example, weighting of the sample to reflect demographic characteristics of the whole population ignores the potential differences between those who have telephones and those who do not. The impact of missing nontelephone households is not critical as long as the topic of the survey is not related directly or indirectly to having a telephone. For other surveys—for example, a poll of the unemployed—this might be a critical difference.

It should always be made clear in reports about telephone sample surveys that the results are representative of all households with telephones—not of the entire country.

It would be possible to take a truly random telephone sample, a completely random digit dialing sample. In this case, the entire telephone number—area code, exchange and suffix—would be generated randomly. The use of random ten-digit numbers would produce a very large number of not working numbers and would not be practical. Fortunately, additional information is available from the telephone company to reduce this error. Telephone company computers can produce a list of working area code/exchange combinations. Only the final four digits of the telephone number are randomly generated, with the knowledge that the random selection of the first six digits will be from working numbers.

This method, standard random digit dialing, is in use today. Even with the assistance of the list from the telephone company, more than three out of four numbers generated are not valid household numbers (Groves et al. 1988:81).

It should also be noted that a correction has to be applied because some households have more than one working telephone number assigned (Groves et al. 1988:81).

Another method of telephone sampling is the use of directories to provide lists of working numbers. In the most simple fashion, randomly or systematically selected numbers from the directories are called directly. This completely misses all unlisted numbers and any numbers assigned since the printing of the directory. With unlisted telephones running to more than half the residences in some cities, this could be a problem.

A variation on this method is to randomly change the last one or two digits of the telephone number selected from the directory. This provides coverage of the unlisted numbers and those that were assigned after printing of the directory.

There are also a number of variants on the random digit dialing method. These include using a sampling scheme that helps to select blocks of numbers with a high density of working household numbers. The Mitofsky–Waksberg two-stage method identifies exchanges with working household numbers; then numbers within those exchanges are used for the second stage (Groves et al. 1988:86). This method can increase the "hit rate" of eligible households from one in four in the first stage to better than six in ten in the second stage (Groves et al. 1988:86).

While the method used to generate a telephone poll sample is too technical to be included in your reporting, it may be important to understand what has been done. Certainly, a survey researcher who cannot explain the sampling methodology to you is subject to question.

SELECTION OF THE RESPONDENT WITHIN A HOUSEHOLD

Even when a selected telephone number is known to be working and that of a household, another aspect of sampling still remains to be done: the interviewer must select the household member to interview. If the person who answered the phone was always selected as the respondent, then teenagers would be very heavily overrepresented in telephone surveys.

Research has demonstrated that samples based just on who answers the telephone are substantially biased, compared with samples in which everyone in the household has a chance to be included.

In order to complete the sampling method, one member of the household needs to be selected. If this is done in a haphazard manner, the sample will potentially have very serious problems.

Leslie Kish developed the most accepted method of respondent selection. This consists of asking the person who answers the phone to complete a list of who lives in the household, and then selecting the respondent based upon a table, known as a Kish table.

A modification of this method, using two simple questions, is also in use. In this case, the person answering the phone is asked how many adults live in the household and then how many female adults. From the answer to these questions, a table can provide the interviewer with the instruction to ask for, say, the oldest female or the second youngest male living in the house.

Other methods have been used to reduce the time and respondent burden of this procedure. One more recent method is the use of the next birthday or last birthday question. Theoretically, this should produce an unbiased sample, but there is at least some evidence that it may oversample females. However, it also may increase response rates (Groves et al. 1988:208).

EXECUTION OF THE SAMPLING METHOD

An early media pollster, who shall remain nameless, often spoke about his sampling techniques—or, rather, the way he bent them to fit his needs. He said that in sampling, the most important thing was to ensure that no respondent lived on an upper floor of a building without an elevator. To him, the effort of climbing stairs was just not worth it. However, respondents on upper floors of buildings without elevators can be different from those on lower floors due to differences in rent.

No sample is any better than the field execution of the sampling design. This is one of the important reasons why experienced survey research companies tend to provide better results; they have had to deal with problems in sample execution, and they work hard to reduce errors. While this makes the survey process more expensive, it also produces better results. A cheap survey that has unknown biases is not worth anything.

WHO DRAWS THE SAMPLE?

Larger survey organizations, particularly those that conduct personal interviews, most often have their own sampling department. Many organizations, large and small, take advantage of the availability of sample vendors. These are organizations of statisticians who take samples for a wide variety of clients. The quality of samples from well-known sample vendors is extremely high, since the samples represent the company's basic product. Use of such samples should never be considered a negative factor in your poll reporting. Remember, however, that precise sample execution is necessary, or the quality of the sample is meaningless.

QUOTA SAMPLING

Prior to 1948, pollsters made the mistake of using quota samples to select the respondents for political surveys. These samples required the interviewer to find a certain number of respondents who were women and a certain number who were men; a certain number who were old, a certain number who were young; and so on. While this produced samples that included the correct number of each of the targeted or quota demographic groups, it did not mean that the sample was representative of the population as a whole.

The major reason for this is that when a deliberate attempt is made to find people of a specific type, the selection process itself may introduce a wide variety of biases. For example, it might be easiest to find people over sixty-five in a residence for the elderly or senior citizen center. But these people are not necessarily representative of those senior citizens who live at home and who work. We might get the correct number of respondents over sixty-five, but they might well be very different from the population we are targeting.

This type of problem also occurs in other demographic groups. Traditionally, it was easier to reach women at home during the day than men. As a result, quota samples for women were often filled by housewives. Working women were harder to contact, so they were often excluded from the sample.

Quota sampling also was a serious problem because of the use of interviewer observation to classify respondents at the same time the interviewer was paid to find respondents who fit certain profiles. Paul Sheatsley, in his inimitable style, related his actions as an early interviewer for the Gallup Organization when quota samples were in use. He recalled that in order to fill the quotas, at the end of the process some respondents represented very unusual combinations of demographic characteristics. Of course, the problems in execution of the sample are not limited to quota samples.

Quota samples are rarely used these days, and only for handling very limited, specific sampling problems. There is no reason to use a quota sample for any general survey of public opinion. Any poll based on a quota sample that crosses a reporter's desk should be carefully scrutinized with the help of polling and sampling experts to determine if this methodology is appropriate for the survey. If the quota sample method is not appropriate, the story should not be written.

CONCLUSION

The details about the sample used for a poll are another set of critical data that is essential to understanding and evaluating the survey. To evaluate a poll well, you must know:

1. How many people were interviewed;
2. How the people interviewed were chosen, both at the household and at the individual level. That is, what type of sampling method was used to select the household and what method was used to select the individual within the household to be interviewed.

To return a third time to the theme, if you cannot obtain this information about a poll, the results of the poll should not be used, reported or referenced. Period.

Chapter 9

THE POLL: THE QUESTIONS

Asking questions lies at the very heart of journalism, for questions are the primary tool each reporter uses to obtain information.

Questions are likewise absolutely critical for public opinion polls, for it is the questions that make up the sum and substance of every survey.

Just as for the journalist, asking the wrong question in a poll will obtain only the wrong answers.

But questions in public opinion polls are quite different in some ways from the questions journalists ask every day in their interviews with sources and public figures. A journalist's questions are designed to elicit information and to generate newsworthy quotes from those who know what the newsperson does not. Often, the journalist is seeking information that the person being questioned doesn't want to give. The journalist's questions are crafted to fit each situation, and perhaps are asked several different ways if the response is not acceptable. A journalist's question can be a challenge, be argumentative or be deceptive—all with the goal of obtaining information.

In public opinion polls, questions are designed to be neutral tools that elicit meaningful responses from many different respondents on a particular subject. Since a poll question may be asked of 2,000 different people, it cannot, and must not, be tailored to any one respondent. A poll is valid only if the same question is asked of all respondents. If each respondent was asked a slightly different question, the poll would be completely invalid. In fact, one of the most important features in training poll interviewers is the absolute rule that the interviewer read the question as written, without any variation. (This is why good journalists make poor poll interviewers: journalists always want to rephrase the question.)

Trying to craft neutral, repeatable questions makes question wording one of the most complex subjects in public opinion polling. Question wording is an art rather than a science. But, fortunately, most of the rules on question wording are common sense.

There is no single right way to ask a question. But the wording of a question will directly impact the results obtained. For that reason, the question wording should be examined at two levels:

Is the question wording so biased, one-sided or difficult that the results should be ignored?

If not, what is the potential impact of the question wording on the results?

In every case, the wording of the question should be known to the journalist, and in the vast majority of cases the complete wording of the question should be included in the story or otherwise made available to the reader or viewer.

IS THE LANGUAGE UNDERSTANDABLE?

As with journalistic writing, the language of questions must be understandable to the audience, the respondents. The first aspect of the question to review is whether the language can be understood by the respondent. Depending upon the group to be surveyed, very technical language might well be included in the question. Just as the language in the *New England Journal of Medicine* is understandable to the readers, so the language in the survey question may well be appropriate for the surveyed population even if it is not understandable to the general population. In these cases, the survey may well be a good one, but you will have a more difficult time reporting the results of the question in a way that is meaningful to the general population.

The problem of difficulty in question language occurs when the question contains words that are not understandable to the population surveyed. This is often the case where specific words within the question are not in common usage, and particularly where the words may sound similar to other words that are more commonly used by the respondents. Questions with this type of problem produce meaningless results, since the interpretation of what the question means is not clear or consistent across respondents. If the question does not appear to be understandable to those surveyed, you should proceed with extreme caution. You might even have to try to ask the question of a few individuals in the population to determine if they understand what the question means.

IS THE QUESTION BALANCED?

The next aspect of the question to check is whether it is balanced. This is more difficult to evaluate, but again, common sense will help.

There is a great deal of controversy over the use of unbalanced questions in polls. Some pollsters use them to measure extremes of opinion; others use two or more unbalanced questions, leaning in opposite directions, to provide a "balanced" picture.

For example, a controversy over the questions asked by Louis Harris revolved around the following types of questions:

1. It is hard to believe that, with his closest associates involved in the Watergate affair, President Nixon did not know about the planning and later cover-up of the affair.
2. He (President Nixon) is being unfairly blamed for things his aides did, which he didn't know about. (Moore 1992:96–97)

These types of projective questions, ones where an opinion is included in the question, can be useful for analysis. However, reporting the results of questions like these is very difficult. How do you compare the results of such biased questions with public opinion measured using balanced questions?

First, the potential of questions like this only underscores the absolute rule that one can never report the results of a poll unless the question wording is known.

Second, the results of any biased or unbalanced question must be placed in context prior to reporting the results. One could say that given even an extreme statement of the facts, some percentage of the people still would support the innocence or guilt of President Nixon. One would have to go on and give the exact question wording, and the results of some other questions that are fair and balanced.

Third, one has to remember that context is important to the respondent as well as to the reader or viewer. This means that some biased questions prior to a balanced one may well impact upon the results. One should therefore be very careful not to report results of a survey where there are one-sided questions followed by balanced questions.

There is another type of unbalanced question that is not at all useful in surveys and should not normally be reported: the loaded question. The difference here is that there is no attempt to balance the survey by including questions biased in both directions.

Loaded questions are often used by advocacy groups to demonstrate support for their positions. Here are some examples that Bradburn and Sudman selected:

> Do you want union officials, in effect, to decide how many municipal employees you, the taxpayer, must support?
> Would you vote for someone who had forced public employees to join a labor union or be fired?
> (Bradburn and Sudman 1988:63–64)

These questions are clearly one-sided. They use language and structure to push the respondent to a specific position. As such, they are interesting to the student of public opinion because they demonstrate the power of the wording of a question. To the journalist, however, they represent a danger, since the results of such questions have been reported as indicative of public opinion.

The majority of these questions will not be reported because the surveys that contain them also have other problems, primarily with sampling and interviewing. However, some questions like these can occur in a survey that is otherwise properly conducted.

It is obviously critical to alert the reader that the question is biased. It is also important to remember that if the biased question cannot be placed into a proper context, it should not be reported.

UNCLEAR QUESTIONS

Sometimes even excellent survey researchers unintentionally word questions in such a way that the respondent is confused. Again, the best method for testing the question is to read it out loud and determine if it seems clear to you.

In some cases, the question is confusing because there are a number of interpretations. Perhaps one of the best examples is from a special study done by the Roper Organization of American opinion on the Holocaust.

In this survey, a number of questions were asked to determine factual knowledge of events at the time of the Holocaust. Results of many of the questions were clear and newsworthy. For example, 38 percent of adults did not know what the Holocaust was or incorrectly explained it, and 22 percent did not know the Nazis first came to power in Germany.

The question that was most widely reported and that was the most difficult to interpret was the following: "Does it seem possible or does it seem impossible to you that the Nazi extermination of the Jews never happened?" Twenty-two percent said it is possible, 65 percent said it is impossible and 12 percent said they didn't know.

But what did those answers mean? First, there is a double negative in the question that may have been very hard for respondents to interpret: does it seem *impossible* that . . . [it] *never* happened.

In addition, there is another potentially serious interpretation problem. After a car accident or other horrible situation, people often say, "It is impossible to believe that it really happened." Perhaps this is also a part of the reason for the answers.

In a letter to colleagues, the Roper Organization acknowledged that the question may well have been confusing. Unfortunately, the reporting of the results occurred prior to the dissemination of the letter.

The press release made the situation worse by combining the "possible" answers with the "don't knows." The release stated that "one third of all adults (34 percent) . . . say either 'it seems possible' . . . or 'don't know.' " This implies that the two groups are somehow related. Lumping the respondents who say they don't know the answer to a question with those who were able to take a position is always tricky, since there can be many reasons for a respondent's inclusion in the "don't know" category.

With this mistake in the press release, the news stories often led with something like "One-third of the population thinks it is possible that the Holocaust never happened or doesn't know." While this was clearly bad reporting, the press release and the poll itself contributed to the problem.

This particular poll was conducted for an advocacy group, the American Jewish Committee, but the intent of the question is not the issue here. The interpretation of the results is the issue. This is a case where the other questions would have provided a reasonably clear picture of opinion, and where the results of this particular question should not have been reported.

Journalists always prefer to have all the information and to make their own decisions on what should and should not be reported. This may well be a case where the public opinion researcher should have included his concerns over the question wording in the information provided to journalists. One does not want to suggest that the question should not have been disclosed to journalists, because one wants to see open disclosure of all the questions in a survey whenever possible. However, it would have been prudent to release the results more carefully.

IF YOU DON'T ASK THE RIGHT QUESTION . . .

One of the problems in questions, in polls and everyday life, is not approaching the topic directly. In some cases, this may be a useful technique to discover information about a topic people are reluctant to discuss, such as drug use or other criminal behavior. In most cases, however, the failure to approach the topic directly is not helpful.

If you want to know if the respondent likes a product or service, it may be interesting to know if he or she uses it regularly, but that doesn't tell you that he or she likes it. All of us may do things we don't like on a regular basis, such as get up for an 8 A.M. class. (Well, maybe on an occasional basis.)

If you don't specifically ask what you want to know, you may not get meaningful results. If the local mayor has just been indicted on child abuse charges, don't ask about the condition of the city when you really want to know if anyone would ever vote for him again. Sometimes these problems are much more subtle. For example, you may find a poll that asks people whether the Senate should ratify a treaty on a certain subject. That is not what the people think about the treaty. If you want to find out public opinion on the treaty, ask it directly: "Do you favor or oppose the . . . ?"

This is important, because the indirect question may bring in spurious influences such as opinion of the Senate, political party dynamics, and even the checks and balances system of the federal government.

USE OF POWERFUL WORDS

Recent research in question wording has again demonstrated that the choice of words is extremely important. If you ask whether or not "The government should *allow* x to happen," when x is controversial, you will get more people to say "No" than the number who would agree that "The government should *prohibit* x from happening." People do not like the idea of the government's prohibiting things, and they like the idea of the government's allowing things. Thus a simple change in the wording, albeit using powerful words, can impact on the results of the question.

These problems crop up particularly in dealing with sensitive subjects, where there is much emotion involved in an individual's views. Questions about abortion, for example, are sensitive to these distinctions, as are questions on homosexuals serving in the U.S. armed forces.

SMALL DIFFERENCES, BIG CHANGES

Both questions and answers are listened to carefully by respondents. Even simple changes in the words used in the answer categories can produce significantly different results.

For example, in the Spring 1989 issue of *Public Opinion Quarterly*, Jon A. Krosnik reported the results of a question wording experiment. In this case, the texts of the question differed only slightly. One-third of the respondents were asked the question with the guidance to tell the interviewer "How acceptable it would be to you personally—very acceptable, somewhat acceptable, not too acceptable or not acceptable at all?" A list of changes in the civil justice system was then read. Another third of the respondents was given the same choices, but with the words "strongly favor, somewhat favor, favor a little or not favor at all." The final third was given the choice of "strongly support, somewhat support, support a little or not support at all."

The results were reported for nine different proposed changes in the judicial system. The experiment demonstrated that there is little difference between "acceptable" and "favor," with the largest observed difference in the positive category of 25 percent and an average difference of 2 percent. However, there was a very significant difference between "support" and the other two. The greatest difference—on a question about placing a cap on the amount that could be collected for pain and suffering—was 63 percent. The average difference was about 30 percent.

Again, it is imperative that you report the actual question wording. This experiment was the result of controversy over the report by the Harris organization of the results of an original survey that used the word "acceptable" in the question. The press reports used "acceptable," "favorable" and "support" interchangeably.

While this may be journalistic license, it is not appropriate in reporting the results of a poll.

ANSWER ORDER

The order in which the possible answers to a question are presented also can create some problems. The easiest examples occur when a respondent is asked to pick one answer from a long list—such as ten possibilities for the most important problem facing the nation. The problem arises because listening to a long list is tiring for the respondent, who has to try to keep all ten concepts in mind while deciding which answer to give. Just as winning the top spot on the ballot can favor a candidate in actual voting, getting the top spot (or the bottom) in a long list of possible answers can skew the results.

With computer-assisted telephone interviewing, this problem can be reduced by rotating the order of the possible answers. Thus, an equal number of respondents hear the list with each item listed first.

An example where rotating order was not possible came in the 1992 national exit poll conducted by Voter Research and Surveys for the television networks. The question asked: "Which one or two issues mattered most in deciding how you voted?" To minimize the order effect, two answer orders were used: in one order on a white ballot and in the reverse order on a yellow ballot. Here are the results (Mitofsky and Edelman 1993:3):

	White	Yellow Reversed Order	Difference
Health Care	24	15	9
Federal Budget Deficit	25	17	8
Abortion	13	11	2
Education	12	13	- 1
Economy/Jobs	41	44	- 3
Environment	4	7	- 3
Taxes	12	17	- 5
Foreign Policy	7	9	- 2
Family Values	10	20	-10

As you can see, the economy/jobs was first on both. But the federal budget deficit and health care were second and third on the white ballot, while family values, taxes and the deficit were second and third on the yellow ballot.

CONCLUSION

No poll can be judged without knowing the exact questions that were asked. As a reporter, you cannot accurately construct a poll story without knowing the questions. You must obtain a copy of the questions asked and the entire questionnaire, if possible. Each question should be evaluated to make certain that the question itself is not distorting the results.

Chapter 10

THE POLL: TIMING IS EVERYTHING

On the night of November 28, 1979, President Jimmy Carter called a news conference in the midst of one of the most agonizing problems ever to face a president: American citizens were being held hostage in the U.S. Embassy in Tehran as extremists threatened dire consequences. Carter's problem was complicated by the dismal view many Americans held of the job he was doing as president, with ratings that rivaled some of the lowest ever seen.

That night, NBC News and The Associated Press were scheduled to conduct the second night of interviews for a national survey of public opinion focusing largely on Carter, the hostages in Iran and similar matters. The raw numbers from the first night of interviewing were not good for Carter: abysmally low job rating, poor marks for the hostage crisis and the like.

With Carter's news conference on the air at 9 P.M., all interviewing was stopped. Like much of the nation, everyone in the polling operation turned to the television to watch Carter as he gave an impassioned plea for freedom for the hostages and a vow that America would stand up to the terrorists.

With the news conference over, the interviewing began again. And what a difference there was!

The public's approval of Carter shot up, and he got high marks for his handling of the hostage crisis from those interviewed after the news conference. In addition, the Americans tapped as respondents wanted to talk, and talk and talk. After answering a question, many of them would say something like "That's not all. I think that . . . "

It was an amazing experience that taught a valuable lesson: exactly when a poll is conducted can make all the difference in the world. The public's view of Carter before the news conference was very different from the opinions after the televised session.

Events can and do have a dramatic impact on poll results. A presidential speech, a stock market crash, an oil spill, a horrible crime, all can sway public attitudes, at least for a time.

Perhaps the best-known examples of this come with presidential approval ratings.

John Mueller first documented the "rally 'round the flag" phenomenon that seems to push up a president's approval ratings in times of crisis. It matters less whether the president has performed well or poorly in the crisis—what is most important is that the nation is gripped by a crisis and the patriotic impulse drives up the president's ratings.

For example, President Kennedy's job ratings rose after the Bay of Pigs invasion, the ill-fated and horribly failed effort to use Cuban exiles as a force to overthrow Cuba's leader, Fidel Castro.

In a much broader way, political scientist Richard Brody's work has demonstrated how events and actions act through the news reports to drive the presidential job ratings.

Thus, the reporting of a poll must include the dates the interviewing was actually conducted. This crucial fact allows everyone to put the poll in some reasonable context.

This is especially true in polls about election campaigns, where the events of a week or even a given day may well change the voters' views of the candidates. Former Colorado senator Gary Hart went from nowhere in the polls to front-runner for the 1984 Democratic presidential nomination within forty-eight hours of his unexpected victory in the New Hampshire primary. Likewise, in 1987, Hart went from front-runner to former candidate in less than a week following revelations of his relationship with model Donna Rice.

MANIPULATION OF POLL TIMING

The sensitivity of poll results to events and new information is now well understood.

Too well understood, in fact, by the political pros who run major election campaigns. An increasingly used tactic is for the campaigns to time their television ads to coincide with a well-known poll's interviewing.

For example, in 1982, Bob Goodman, a GOP consultant, was working for Pete Wilson in his bid for the U.S. Senate. Wilson, then the mayor of San Diego, faced a field of fellow Republicans in the primary, including one carrying one of the most significant names in the party—Barry Goldwater, Jr. Up against such a well-known name, Wilson felt he had to show strength in the early polls.

After that campaign, Goodman said that they found out when the California Poll by Field Research was going to do its interviews. And the campaign took advantage of that small piece of information: its television ad buys were timed to the poll interviewing. "We backdated our whole [time buying] to two weeks before the Field Polls. We knew that if we didn't go from 12% to 14% and then 14% to 18% and then 18% to 22%, our money would have dried up and we'd be out of the game" (Rothenberg 1983: 11). The Wilson campaign advertised right before each wave of California Poll interviewing, his poll standings rose, his fund-raising went well and he went on to win a seat in the U.S. Senate.

FIRM OPINIONS VERSUS FIRST IMPRESSIONS

More and more in the last decade, the news media have conducted surveys right on the heels of news events.

Early examples of these polls were the post-debate surveys conducted immediately after the Carter–Ford presidential debates in 1976. Such "instant polls," roundly criticized at the time, have become a staple of presidential campaign coverage. There is wide variation in the quality of the quick polls. The best are so-called panel-back surveys that talk to respondents before an event and then interview the same people after the event. This technique provides an excellent method of gauging the changes in opinion in response to events. It is less useful in providing an accurate picture of the current, overall state of public opinion.

There is a serious practical difficulty in many instant polls because the events people are evaluating occur late in the day or in the evening. It is difficult to interview a new, proper sample when you begin after 10 P.M. on the East Coast.

The instant polls raise another kind of question: Do they tap the genuine opinions of people or just the "off-the-top-of-my-head" reactions from people who have had little or no time to think, reflect and consider developments?

There is no simple answer.

Quick reactions to well-understood events involving well-known figures—such as an American president—are shaped not only by the most recent event but also by the much longer series of presidential actions, speeches and policies that form a strong foundation for a judgment.

Where the participants are not well known, or where the event is still unfolding, the analysis of an instant poll must be much more tentative.

In addition, public opinion is shaped by the reaction to and the analysis of following events from the news media and one's fellow citizens. This phenomenon has been seen repeatedly with presidential campaign debates.

President Gerald Ford committed one of the more memorable gaffes in his face-off with Jimmy Carter in 1976. In answer to a question, Ford said that Poland was not dominated by the Soviet Union. At the time, Poland was firmly in the control of a Communist government closely linked to Moscow.

The Associated Press was conducting a panel-back survey on that debate, which allowed the addition of response categories to a question on high points or mistakes during the debate. Less than 1 percent of those questioned mentioned Ford's gaffe immediately after the debate.

But two days later—after Ford's gaffe had been spread across the front pages of many newspapers and the television news, a Harris poll found most Americans aware of the gaffe and unhappy with Ford for the mistake.

This phenomenon is also responsible for a "bandwagon" effect on the question of who wins these televised debates. In 1984, 1988 and 1992, polls concerning who won the presidential debates often showed a consistent pattern. The candidate judged the winner of the debate in the first polls after the event—even if quite narrowly—would be declared the winner of the debate by wider and wider margins in polls conducted more and more days after the debate.

"OLD POLLS"

With "instant polls," tracking polls and the rapid response now featured in the news media, the opposite question about poll timing is also important: If a poll was not conducted recently, is it still news, is it still valid?

The answer varies by what the poll covers.

If the poll matches the Democratic and Republican candidates for president, a poll conducted in early September of the election year is not very valuable if it is not released until late October. After nearly two months of campaigning, paid ads and much news coverage, too much has changed to make those September numbers on the presidential race newsworthy or meaningful, except to historians.

Conversely, poll questions on issues that are not usually subject to wide fluctuation are valuable long after the poll is conducted. For example, polls on religious beliefs and church attendance are valid for months, because these are matters that change little, if at all, over a few months.

In addition, certain types of scholarly work can be newsworthy even if the poll is many months old.

The National Election Survey (NES) and the General Social Survey (GSS) are two of the benchmark studies that provide a series of polls over the last forty years, providing a depth and breadth of information on opinion trends and changes that can be quite interesting. It is less important that some of the NES polls on the election are not released until months after the balloting. It is more important what the polls show about the trends in the American electorate.

CONVERSELY

The importance of knowing when a poll was conducted has a corollary that is not quite so obvious.

Two polls by the same firm, using the same questions in successive months, should provide a reliable gauge of the changes—or the lack of changes—in public opinion. If two quite similar polls separated in time give different results, there should be a reason for the difference.

As discussed above, public opinion changes for a reason. Our views of the president, of the world, of whatever are driven by what we know, what we talk about, what we learn. In the realm of public policy, the actions or inactions of public officials are often the news that helps drive public opinion.

Conversely, if there is no obvious reason that public opinion should have moved—and it appears to have moved—a big red warning flag should go up. If two similar polls separated in time have different results without any obvious reason for the change, it's time to look at those polls very carefully to see if there are technical reasons the numbers changed.

Is the base of respondents the same in both polls—for example, does one use all Americans and one only registered voters? Did the questions change in a subtle but significant way? Was the interviewing done on weekdays in one poll and over a weekend in the other?

CONCLUSION

Before analyzing a poll, you must know when the interviews were conducted. This fact helps you place the poll results in context. A poll without interviewing dates should be treated simply: it should be ignored.

Chapter 11

THE POLL: SAMPLING ERROR

Now we know a lot about this particular poll: Who conducted the poll, who sponsored it, what the sample was like, what questions were asked and when it was taken. All of that information is important in evaluating the survey results and in deciding whether you want to report it. But you have to remember that no matter how good the survey, there will always be some error.

This is not only error in the sense of "We made a mistake." This error includes the reality that we did not talk to everyone in the population, and thus we acknowledge the likelihood that the poll results may not match the true opinions of the entire population exactly.

The most commonly reported source of error in surveys is sampling error. The major reason why this error is reported so often is that it is simple to calculate and takes little time or space to report.

The sampling error figure for a poll should be provided by the polling firm that conducted the poll.

What is sampling error? It should be obvious to you that taking a sample entails some risks of getting a group that is not representative of the population as a whole. Even a perfectly drawn and executed sample can produce a subset of the population that does not accurately reflect the population as a whole.

For example, if you sample registered voters in a specific city, you will often get a proportion of Democrats that is larger or smaller than the total in the population. This is due to the chance variation between samples. The sample error is the amount of chance variation expected in a series of samples of the population. It is extremely important to remember that what we are calling sample error is present in a perfectly correct sample; we are talking about random chance here, not mistakes in taking or executing a sample.

The variation of the results of a sample is dependent upon two basic, easily measurable criteria: the size of the sample and the size of the population. For most of our surveys, the size of the population is so large that it does not impact upon the error calculation. This is true unless the sample is greater than 25 percent of the population in size (Bradburn and Sudman 1988:182). The size of the sample is the key variable in the calculation of sampling error.

If you took a group of samples from the same population in the same way, the results of the samples would be distributed around the result that would occur if you had taken a census of the population. Remember, we are considering only the errors produced by sampling alone, no consideration is given to other possible problems. Statisticians have produced a method to estimate the variation around the actual result in the population for samples of different sizes. It is this variation that is called sample error.

The normal way this variation is expressed is as a measure of the precision of the results from a sample. For example, most of the better-known national polls report a sample error of plus or minus 3 percentage points. What does this mean?

The survey organization is reporting that based on variation in sampling alone, the chances are 95 out of 100 or better that the results of this survey are within 3 percentage points of the results if a census had been taken using the same method. This means that if you have a result, say 45 percent of the public support candidate A, the actual result is likely to be from 42 percent to 48 percent. We can even estimate how likely: 95 percent of the time, since the sampling error was stated in that way.

Figure 11.1 represents a graphical depication of the sampling error in a survey. The bulk of the possibilities fall in the middle of the curve; in fact, 95 percent do.

Figure 11.1

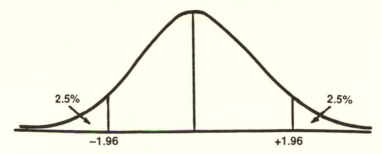

This curve, called a normal distribution, has some very important known characteristics. For our purposes, the most important property is that 95 percent of all the cases under the curve fall within a specified distance from the average. This distance turns out to be 1.96 units of standard error. The calulation of standard error is beyond the scope of this book.

This also means that 2.5 percent of the cases are further above the average and 2.5 percent are further below the average. The remaining 95 percent represent the results within the sampling error. The remaining results, the 5 percent that are further away from the average represent the one chance in 20 that a poll result is outside the margin of error.

For some studies, a 95 percent range is not good enough. When you are talking about mortality rates from a new drug, you might want to be a little more careful and look at a more extensive range of variation, say 99 percent or 99.9 percent or even 99.999 percent. In each of these cases, if the sample size does not change, the estimated range of sampling error will increase.

So the number we report, the sampling error, is an estimate of the size of the range of the results we have to consider to be reasonably certain, usually 95 percent certain, that the results in the population fall within the selected range.

So far we have only considered the size of the sample and the population. Remember that we are also only considering the error produced by random chance. To be even more precise, we have to look at the results of the survey because they can impact on the calculation of sampling error.

Table 11.1
Sample Sizes and Sampling Errors Rounded up to next 5

Confidence Interval 95%				
Size of Population Assumed Prevalence = 50%	+ /- 1%	+ / - 2%	+ /- 3%	+ /- 4%
1,000	*	*	*	375
10,000	4900	1935	965	570
100,000	8765	2345	1060	600
>500,000	9425	2390	1065	600
Assumed Prevalence < 15% or > 85%				
1,000	*	*	355	235
10,000	3290	1095	520	300
100,000	4670	1210	545	305
>500,000	4850	1225	545	310

*Sample required is more than 50% of the population. Method of sample error calculation is not accurate at those sampling rates.

If you are measuring a very rare attribute of the population, say an opinion that only one person in 100 holds, you are not as likely to be very far off as you are if you measure something that occurs in about half the population. (Incidentally, the same is true if you are measuring something that occurs in almost all the population.)

It is easy to see how you might be off a lot if something is present in 50 percent of the population. It would be very easy, by chance, to select a few more or less who have the characteristic. But if only 5 percent of the population have it, or if 95 percent do, the chance of being off a lot is reduced.

This is for two reasons. First, it is hard to get too many of those who are rare in the population because they are rare. Second, you cannot ever have enough measurement error so that the results of your sample demonstrate more than 100 percent or less than 0 percent.

For example, in a random sample of 1,000 out of a large population, the sampling error to give you 95 percent confidence is 1 percent if the characteristic is shown by either 5 percent or 95 percent of the population and 3 percent if the characteristic is shown by 50 percent (Fowler 1993:31). Sampling error in polls is normally reported at the 50 percent distribution, the highest potential chance for error, so that sampling error is not understated.

As a journalist, you do not have to report the range of sampling errors for each potential distribution in the population; the maximum sampling error is sufficient.

It is important to report sampling error in a meaningful way. Many readers do not understand a statement such as the following: "The results of this poll are subject to a sampling error of plus or minus 3 percentage points." While that statement is accurate, it is neither complete nor clear. The story must go on to explain at least a bit of what that means. A frequent formulation used by The Associated Press is to say the poll is subject to sampling error and then to add: "That is, if one could talk to all adults in the country there is only one chance out of twenty that results would vary from the findings of this poll by more than three percentage points simply because of sample error."

You have to recognize that this potential error is present in each and every poll. Too often the story does not seem even to consider any margin for error. In fact, often the story gives the poll an aura of accuracy that is not deserved.

Newspaper stories that use poll results are often followed by little boxes that remind readers of the poll's margin of error and explain what it means. The electronic media often mention the "plus or minus" aspect of a result in passing. However, this acknowledgment of the inherent imprecision of poll data is often little more than a footnote—a footnote overshadowed by a story that treats the results as if they were chiseled in granite. (Lavrakas and Holley 1991:189)

In broadcasting, it is much more difficult to include any real discussion of error margins and what they mean. Because of the time constraints and the resultant limitations on the number of words available, most broadcast media at best report the sampling error with a simple statement or by including a graphic display of plus or minus some number in the visual portion of the report.

While this may not provide a significant portion of the audience with enough information to understand what sampling error means, most of the media do provide press releases about their own polls that contain more extensive information about sampling error and other methodological questions.

However, it is clear that broadcast media have a very difficult time reporting on sampling error and other methodological details of the poll. For this reason, they may have to make an even greater effort to avoid the implication in the story that the poll results are absolute, numbers that are not subject to error.

Finally, in reporting sampling error in polls, it is most important not to give the impression that this is the only error in the polling process. Bud Roper, longtime chairman of the Roper Organization, a past president of AAPOR and a trustee of the National Council on Public Polls, has warned for more than a decade that the use of sampling error or margin of error as the only reported estimate of error leads the public to the erroneous conclusion that the poll is entirely accurate except for the margin of error. This is certainly incorrect, and not the impression that you want to leave with your readers or audience. Many poll stories now contain a disclaimer which indicates that sampling error is only one of the many sources of error in public opinion polling, and that every survey is subject to other practical difficulties.

We have already discussed the impact of questions on the results. In the next chapter we will talk about some of the other sources of error that can impact on poll results.

Chapter 12

THE POLL: OTHER SOURCES OF ERROR

Since the beginning of modern public opinion research, pollsters like Gallup, Roper, and Crossley were well aware that the results of their surveys could be significantly affected by the way in which questions were worded, by the format in which they were presented, and by the order and context in which they were asked. (Bishop and Smith 1993:1)

Sampling error is the caveat that almost every news story about a poll now includes, whether in print or on the air.

But there are many, many other possible sources of error in every poll. Many of these possible errors can't be neatly quantified in a nice round number. Many of them are quite subtle, even with all the information about a poll at hand.

In this chapter, we turn to a variety of other problems that can bedevil polls and how to deal with them.

QUESTION ORDER

Pollster Peter Hart suggests that "Placement of questions can really determine what the results of asking a question will be" (Cantril 1980:62). In many instances, questions about a candidate's weaknesses precede a hypothetical vote question and significantly lower the candidate's support.

This is also true of other measures. For example, presidential popularity can be influenced by asking a question about economic conditions immediately before. In times of good economic conditions, the presidential popularity will be increased; in times of poor economic conditions, the presidential popularity will be reduced.

There are times when the order effects can be more subtle. If a questionnaire is designed with a series of questions about one specific candidate prior to an electoral test question, the impact can be to distort the results one way or another, depending upon the impression left by the questions. Sometimes, a specific question may increase support among one group while reducing it among another.

The only easy test for you is to read the questionnaire as administered, to determine if the questions before the one you are reporting seem to have a potential impact. In that case, you need to report the results with a caveat about prior questions in the questionnaire.

It may be that the polling firm will not release the entire questionnaire. This can often be a reasonable action because there may be questions from more than one client on the same poll. In that case, the other clients might not want the questions that they ask to be made publicly available even without results. If the company is a quality one, it will attempt to let you look at the preceding questions with an agreement that you will not report them. If not, the pollster may tell you the content of the preceding questions without revealing the specific questions. You will have to determine what to report about such a situation. Normally, unless there is some reason to suspect that the order effect will be substantial, knowledge of the subject matter of the preceding questions is sufficient.

NONRESPONSE

Nonresponse bias, the failure of one group to respond in the same proportions as another, is a very important problem in public opinion polling. This has been true since the advent of straw polls.

In the 1936 *Literary Digest* fiasco, not all the problems were sampling related. In fact, Democratic voters failed to return ballots more often than Republican voters did.

In some locations, the *Digest*'s sampling frame did not consist of telephone and automobile lists, but voter registration lists. In Allentown, Pennsylvania, for example, the *Digest* mailed ballots to all registered voters. Thus each voter has an equal chance of being included in the poll (a 100 percent chance), and there was no sampling bias. However, there was an obvious response bias. (Moore 1992:52)

The results of the poll overstated Landon's support by twelve percentage points, clearly the result of response bias, not sampling error.

With similar results elsewhere when an unbiased sample was used, the *Literary Digest* demonstrated clearly that nonresponse can really spoil the pollster's day.

MEASURING NONRESPONSE

Nonresponse is perhaps the most inscrutable of survey errors. Many other survey errors can, at least theoretically, be dealt with if the researcher has adequate financial and administrative resources. Nonresponse in voluntary surveys, however, is the result of behavior of persons who are outside the researcher's control. (Groves et al. 1988:191)

Perhaps one of the most difficult areas for a journalist to measure is nonresponse. This is primarily due to the failure of most survey organizations to report response rates. With the possible exception of very expensive government-sponsored surveys, few polls, if any, reach very high levels of response rates. Because most surveys have a short field period, and because most polls are conducted for a limited amount of money, low response rates are the norm.

In many cases, the calculation of response rates is not clear. When a number is called but the phone is not answered, even after a number of callbacks, is that a lost respondent? While it may seem that it is, there are a number of phone systems in the country that fail to provide an operator interrupt when the number is no longer in service. In addition, if the field period does not include daytime hours, the number might belong to a business and therefore not be eligible for inclusion in the survey.

The same problem can be true for numbers that are continuously busy.

Most quality survey research organizations can estimate the nonresponse rate for a given survey for you. They not only will give you a rate but also will provide information about other similar surveys to help you put the response rate into perspective.

COPING WITH NONRESPONSE

Unless the sponsor of the survey is willing to spend a great deal of time and money tracking down and convincing the nonrespondents, there is no effective way to wipe out the nonresponse. Many studies have been done to determine the impact of longer field periods for interviewing. But a longer field period runs the risk that major news events can occur in the middle of the survey. That can have a very important impact on the results. Researchers have also looked at the results of more calls to a specific number, attempting to locate those who are hard to reach.

All of these attempts can provide some insight as to the kinds of people who are less likely to participate in a survey. But what can be done to correct the results, to adjust for nonresponse?

The true answer is "very little." Most survey organizations already adjust the results of surveys for demographic imbalances in the sample. This is the process known as weighting. If, for example, the population surveyed has 30 percent males over twenty-five, the results of the survey can be adjusted so that males over twenty-five represent exactly 30 percent of the opinions. Multiple adjustments can be made so that the demographics of the weighted sample closely resemble the population.

However, this type of adjustment does not provide real correction for nonresponse unless those who respond within a demographic group are exactly the same as those who did not respond in terms of their opinions on the questions asked. There is no reason to believe that this is true.

Depending upon the circumstances, it may be more realistic to assume that those who do not respond differ significantly from those who did. Fortunately, in American public opinion, for the most part this is not the case. While research shows that there is often a difference between the two groups, in most cases the difference is small and does not have a very significant impact on the outcome of the survey.

The most important issue to remember here is that if a particular survey is on a topic that appears to be related to any reason for nonresponse, you should be exceptionally careful to review the response rate and to insert a caution into your story about the results. This might be the case in an emotionally charged racial election where nonresponse might be disproportionate in a minority community. Or it might be in a survey of attitudes toward poor people, the homeless or some other group less likely to respond to the survey.

BACKGROUND NOISE

In any survey, you should remember that people express opinions on subjects about which they know nothing. Of course, that is their right in a democracy, and they may well have an important impact on the political process even on those subjects. However, in reporting poll results, you should be careful about results on topics that are not well known. We know that people will tell us their opinions of political issues that do not even exist. For example, Bishop et al. reported that without any prior questioning of knowledge on a fictitious law, one-third of the respondents expressed an opinion favoring or opposing a repeal. When first asked a question about whether or not they knew about the act, had been interested enough in the act, or had thought about the act, these numbers dropped to less than 8 percent (Bishop et al. 1980:201).

This means that unless some attempt is made to evaluate the level of information about a subject, a significant segment of the public may well express an opinion without any real knowledge or consideration. There are those commentators who say this is the way elections are also conducted; after all, no one is questioned on his or her level of knowledge about the candidates prior to voting.

INTERVIEWER-CAUSED ERRORS

The best questionnaires possible, administered to the best sample possible, may not produce meaningful results if the interviewers don't do their job. The entire process of surveys is dependent upon the interaction between the interviewer and the respondent. While there have been many attempts to reduce this dependency, for telephone and personal interviewing, the interviewer is a key component of the survey system.

This is not true for mail surveys and other self-administered questionnaires, such as intercept kiosks and machine-conducted surveys. While mail surveys can produce acceptable results, the kiosk and machine polls have serious problems associated with them.

In the vast majority of surveys you will evaluate, interviewers play a key role. This means that they must understand how to administer the questionnaire, how to select respondents, how to record the answers, how to answer questions from respondents, and how to interact with respondents in general. This process requires training of interviewers, one of the most often neglected phases of a quality research project.

While many major survey research firms recruit and train a staff of interviewers who work on a long-term basis, other companies hire interviewers for a specific project and may train them on the job. This is another reason to look carefully at the research company conducting the survey.

The interviewer training process is most important where there are volunteer or student interviewers. In these cases, it is extremely important to ask about the interviewer training process.

Interviewers can also suffer from a bias for or against a position or candidate. Again, this is most important in volunteer interviewers, since they are likely to volunteer when they have an interest in the outcome of the project. In many cases, interviewers with strongly held positions can produce biased results without any conscious effort, just by the way they react to answers or how they read questions. Be extremely careful of any survey where the interviewers have a point of view.

Interviewers make other mistakes because of a lack of understanding or knowledge, or deliberate attempts at distortion or fraud. In order to ensure that the process is correctly followed, most survey houses will monitor telephone interviewers to be sure that they ask the correct questions the correct way. This may find simple errors, such as pronunciation of names, or incorrect use of skip patterns. It also may find interviewers who are discussing the questions with the respondents.

Monitoring is most difficult with in-person interviewing. Because of this, most personal interviewers complete a more extensive training program. However, they still have more freedom in the field that can produce problems. To detect outright fraud or deception, respondents may be called by supervisors to ensure that they have been interviewed, that the interview took place on the date and at the time recorded by the interviewer and that certain key questions have been correctly reported. This can also be used to verify results in telephone interviewing where monitoring is either not available or not extensive.

Interviewers do make mistakes. Some errors occur despite the use of proper training and supervision. However, the number of errors increases greatly when untrained, unsupervised interviewers are used.

DATA PROCESSING ERRORS

Information in surveys is gathered either by listening or by having people complete a questionnaire themselves. The problems in recording of correct responses is part of the error that can be introduced by the interviewer. However, even if the correct information is recorded on paper, it may not be correctly entered into the computer. To reduce this problem, a number of computer techniques have evolved, including Computer-Assisted Telephone Interviewing (CATI) and Computer-Assisted Personal Interviewing (CAPI). These provide the interviewer with a computer or computer terminal upon which to record the results of each question. These techniques not only reduce errors in reading the responses but also provide for control over the skip patterns in the questionnaire. Skip patterns are used to change the questions asked on the basis of the results of prior questions. For example, if the respondent is not registered to vote, you may not want to ask other questions about voting, but you may want to ask questions about views on the economy. With the computer to assist, the correct question will appear automatically, changing the reliance on the interviewer's work.

However, this introduces the potential for errors in computer processing to change the skip patterns. While such problems should be found in the pretesting phase of the survey, they have been known to exist in projects in the field.

Other data processing problems are more likely to impact on the results. Most are due to simple errors. For example, the wording for a specific question that is listed in the computer might not match what is actually on the questionnaire. In that case, the analyst looking at the results might reach a totally incorrect conclusion. This has occurred during Election Night analysis of results of exit polls where the analysis system did not contain the same questions that were on the questionnaire. For most analysts, this type of error is obvious once analysis begins.

Another problem of a similar nature is the conversion of responses from open-ended questions to specific answer categories. While this process is outside the scope of this book, there is the potential for significant error to be introduced in the coding and recording of answers to open-ended questions.

A variety of other problems in data processing can also cause errors from data conversion utilities to recoding and weighting processes. It is not likely that a journalist will have access to the information required to evaluate the quality of the data processing. However, it is another example of errors not covered by the error margin and is certainly an area to look at if results appear to be suspect.

Chapter 13

PSEUDO-POLLS AND SLOPS

Perhaps the most serious development in the reporting of polls has been the emergence of worthless, useless and misleading pseudo-polls. Pseudo-polls are those that are not based upon scientific samples.

The most common forms of these are the call-in and the mail-in coupon polls. Dr. Norman Bradburn, former director of the National Opinion Research Center has described these types of endeavors as SLOPS, Self-selected Listener-Oriented Public opinion Surveys.

In this book, such surveys will be called SLOPS, which is indicative of the total and complete lack of reliability in them.

The most common SLOPS is the call-in poll. In its most common version, a question is posed that can be answered with yes or no, and two telephone numbers are given. The number of calls to the "yes" number are tallied as "yes" responses and the number of calls to the "no" number are tallied as "no" responses. The totals are then expressed as a percentage.

This type of SLOPS is seductive because the number of responses can be huge, in the hundreds of thousands. It can also be a major revenue source, since there normally is a fee for each call.

The other major type of SLOPS is the coupon mail-in poll. In this type, a newspaper or magazine publishes a coupon that contains one or more questions. In order to respond, the individual returns the coupon either via mail or, with the advent of modern technology, via fax. In some cases, the responses are made via electronic mail.

Again, the potential number of responses can be so large as to provide a façade of reliability. It is hard to ignore SLOPS that report the results of 200,000 responses.

The major problem with SLOPS is that you have absolutely no idea whether the results have any projectability to the population in question. In Chapter 8 we discussed the importance of scientific samples so that the journalist knows the results represent something about the population in question. When you have no idea who is included in the sample, there is absolutely no way you can evaluate the results other than to throw them away.

SLOPS have no value except for entertainment.

SLOPS are perfectly appropriate to help "Saturday Night Live" determine whether or not to eat Larry the Lobster, and they may be fine to determine which quarterback is the best of all time on the Saturday afternoon sports show. However, it is important even in these cases to remember that the results are fun, interesting and meaningless.

During the 1992 election, *The New York Times* reported the results of one of these polls, tongue in cheek. On October 27, 1992, on page B6, an article reported the results of the "Kydes Poll." *The Times* said, "Chris Kydes has his fingers on the electorate's souls—and soles."

Mr. Kydes is a cobbler who keeps the tally on a pad next to the cash register. His prediction in 1992 was a Bush victory. The methodology section of the report included the following:

> All customers were asked: "If you had to vote right now, who'd you pick, Bush, Clinton or Perot?" Those who said they were undecided were informed, "Nope, Can't. No undecideds allowed."
>
> The potential sampling error for a poll of this kind is incalculable. In theory, in 99 polls of this kind, the results would be incorrect 99 times. In reality, in four similar previous polls, the cobbler was always right.

Of course, reporting of these polls in this way is acceptable. One hopes that both readers and editors will recognize the character of the story and react accordingly.

There are a number of circumstances where SLOPS and real polls have been done on the same subject at the same time. These are very important because they can give us some insight into the differences.

In 1987, ABC News asked the same question on a 900-number poll and a scientific poll: Should the United Nations headquarters stay in the United States?

	Phone-in Poll	**Scientific Poll**
	100,000+ callers	500+ respondents
Yes	33%	66%
No	67%	25%
Don't Know		9%

After the Carter-Reagan debate in 1980, ABC News sponsored a call-in poll. Respondents dialed one number to vote for Carter as the winner, another for Reagan as the victor in the televised debate. It cost each caller 50 cents. More than 727,000 calls were recorded, and Reagan was the winner by a 2–to-1 margin. *The New York Post* trumpeted the poll in a giant front-page headline proclaiming a big GOP win.

But it was just wrong. An AP poll taken at the same time found that the viewers were evenly split between the incumbent president and his Republican challenger.

Well after the election, campaign staffers from both the Reagan and the Carter camps would admit that they knew of the ABC call-in poll in advance and had their campaign volunteers ready at banks of telephones. The Reagan phone banks were apparently better at getting through than the Carter phone banks.

The major conclusion that can be drawn from these cases is that we really don't know what the results mean with SLOPS. Large numbers don't mean anything at all; the *Literary Digest* should be your guideline whenever SLOPS is presented to you for reporting.

The most difficult problem of SLOPS is caused by their use in otherwise professional news reporting situations. Most often they are used by local news programs where the question is posed on the early news and the results reported on the late news.

For many different reasons, SLOPS continue to be used by news organizations. In response to direct questioning, many organizations respond that they conduct a SLOPS to "enhance interaction with readers" or viewers. This is often the case presented for using fax polls in magazines. In addition, the editors often say that they use the results to assist them in finding story ideas. Both of these reasons are valid, as long as the results of the SLOPS are not reported. Once the results are reported, these arguments no longer hold.

It is important to remember that greater damage can be done by the secondary reporting of these SLOPS. Even those that are done in fun are sometimes picked up and reported as real poll results.

One famous SLOPS was conducted by a toilet tissue manufacturing company in the Midwest in 1976, during the presidential election. Rolls of toilet tissue were printed with the image of either Jimmy Carter or Gerald Ford. The company totaled the number of rolls sold with each candidate's picture and reported the results, tongue in cheek, in a press release in which the methodology was clearly disclosed.

Initial reporting of the press release was also humorous, but the story soon appeared on a wire service as the results of a poll taken in the Midwest, without any of the methodological information. This story was then included along with real polls in roundups of recent poll results.

Thus, the most important problem with SLOPS is the failure to apply the standards of reporting that should be applied to all polls. Since SLOPS have no meaning, they should never be included in a story except for entertainment value, and the reporter and editor must be very careful to ensure that they do not slip into news stories.

Chapter 14

REPORTING POLLS: THE BASICS

The poll results are in hand, and they look good from a technical point of view. Now the challenge is to turn the numbers into a readable story for the morning newspaper or a compelling piece for the evening news.

Just as there are good polls and bad polls, there are good stories based on polls and bad stories based on polls. Even the best poll can be grossly misinterpreted, dramatically misrepresented or just garbled by a poorly done story in the newspaper or on the television news show.

From the journalist's perspective, a poll should be just another source of information, a source with limitations, potential problems and biases, but a valuable source nonetheless.

The problems with news stories on polls arise from a number of areas:

Journalists writing about polls lack the basic understanding of polling to interpret the numbers accurately.

Journalistic values of speed, freshness, conflict and objectivity conspire to push poll stories too far.

Journalists love numbers. Numbers, especially those wrapped in the scientific method, are "truth" to many journalists. They are concrete, they are solid, not subject to all the problems of just getting the information from a human being.

With such an attitude, journalists can often fall into the trap of treating poll results as gospel, as the "unquestionable reality" of public opinion. One of the points of this book is to try to break such habits among journalists and replace them with a more reasoned and sophisticated understanding of polls and the uses of polls.

Another journalistic trait often threatens the good reporting of polls: the tendency to grab for the biggest headline possible. Use the biggest number possible, drop all the caveats and aim for the front page.

Sometimes the results of this journalistic urge are simply funny.

In September 1979, AP and NBC News conducted a poll of Catholics in advance of Pope John Paul's first visit to the United States. Catholics, the poll said, tended to disagree with the pope and their church's doctrines on a number of significant issues: abortion, birth control, women priests and the like. *The New York Post* liked the story so much that it gave it a big headline: "Catholics in Poll Shocker!"

Some people may have been shocked at the poll results. But it was no surprise to American Catholics and to anyone who followed public opinion in the 1970s that Catholics' views on these issues were not very different from those of the public as a whole. And certainly the heated debates among the church faithful that attracted major attention for years should have made these poll results interesting—if not exactly a "shocker."

Unfortunately, this sensationalist urge can lead to bad poll stories.

ANALYZING THE POLL

A journalist analyzing a poll for a news story is quite different from an academic researcher looking at the same poll. The main difference is that the journalist must look for the news in the survey results: what is new, what has changed, what is surprising, what has the most support among the public—or the most opposition. The academician is looking for something quite different: what information the poll adds to the existing knowledge about the topic at hand.

Another key difference is that the journalist has at most a day or two to do the poll analysis, write the story and shepherd it through the editing process. Under some circumstances—Election Night, for instance—the journalist may have only hours or minutes to analyze the data and put the story together. The academician has months. The journalist's task also varies depending on how much information is available from the poll.

If the survey was conducted by the newspaper, television station or radio station, the newsperson should have reams of computer printouts, with hundreds of tables providing many, many different ways to look at the results. In this case, the journalist must do a primary analysis of the data. This means sitting down with the printouts—or at a computer with access to the data—and looking through each question and each crosstabulation of the questions. This takes time, intellectual energy and dedication. And it is the only way to analyze a poll well.

Most polls that come across a journalist's desk are from outside groups—polling firms, other news organizations, special interest groups, foundations and the like. In this case, much less information is readily available to the journalist than if the news organization did the poll. The reams of computer printouts are probably not provided (although they should be available if you need them).

What comes with these polls in place of an inch-thick stack of printouts is an analysis of the poll results done by the polling firm or the group that sponsored the poll. This is both helpful and dangerous.

It is helpful because someone else has already gone through the reams of printouts and provided a look at what is interesting or meaningful in the results. Much of the data from many polls is only vaguely interesting from a news perspective—although it might be fascinating and quite valuable for a political campaign, a marketing company or an academic researcher. That someone else has already looked at the data and distilled it for you saves a great deal of time.

The predigested analysis is also dangerous.

A poll's sponsor is going to highlight in the analysis and the press release the findings that are consistent with the sponsor's views. Not that the analysis will always be deceptive, but it will emphasize what the sponsor thinks is interesting. And what the sponsor thinks is interesting is not necessarily the news.

For example, an environmental group might release a poll that shows two-thirds of the public says that they themselves are environmentalists and that the government should do more to clean up the environment. But the interesting result may be that the self-described environmentalists are opposed to paying higher taxes to help clean up the nation's water supply.

Legitimate poll sponsors will provide enough information about the survey results to allow you to do some secondary analysis of the data. For example, the sponsor should provide a copy of the questionnaire with the results of each question . With this, you can look through all the questions, not just the ones highlighted in the press release.

Whether you have reams of printouts or just the press release, questionnaires and some tables of numbers, the analysis process for the journalist has the same goals.

You are looking for the most interesting data in the survey. What is the result that makes you stop and say, "I didn't know that's what people think"? What are the numbers that are the most revealing about the current state of public opinion? In analyzing the data, always look carefully at the questions with two kinds of results:

1. Those where a clear majority supports one view.
2. Those where public opinion is evenly split.

Both types of results can provide good material for the news story. Results with a clear majority are relatively easy to write and easy for the reader or the viewer to understand. The questions with roughly even divisions are usually those tapping the sources of greatest conflict in the public debate. Conflict is often the grist for good news stories. But don't forget that there is often a value in reporting results that confirm general expectations, or that reaffirm that views have not changed.

YOU HAVE A THEORY, WHETHER YOU KNOW IT OR NOT

One of the points that Phil Meyer makes in *Precision Journalism* is that journalists refuse to acknowledge that they come to a poll—or another set of data—with a theory about what they will find.

Having a theory to prove or disprove is the very foundation of the scientific method. No scientist or social scientist would dare attempt an analysis of data without starting with the theory of what is there.

But starting with a theory makes journalists very, very nervous. This sounds like bias. It sounds like a preconceived notion. It sounds like the journalist lacks objectivity. All bad things from the journalist's perspective.

But a theory is not only not bad, it is essential for the journalist. On top of that, every journalist who analyzes a poll has a theory he or she is trying to prove or disprove. The theory may be unspoken and unacknowledged, but it is there.

The theory may be as simple as "Walter Mondale looked great in that debate and President Reagan looked terrible. Is that what the viewers saw during the debate?" That's a perfectly good theory, and it is one that can be tested with an appropriately designed poll.

Or the theory may be that the president's job rating has skyrocketed because of the success of the war against Iraq. Again, a simple, testable theory.

Journalists need to understand the importance of the theory with which they start their analysis on each poll—even if it is proven totally incorrect!

WRITING THE STORY

You've pored over the printouts, you know what is interesting, you know what is surprising in the results—now you have to turn that into a news story. How to approach this task varies, of course, depending on the medium: a 90-second television piece is quite different from a 1,200-word newspaper story. Even so, there are some basic guidelines for writing the story that will help.

1. What's the lede? This is not just literally what is in the first paragraph of the story. This is what is the most important poll finding, what is most interesting. What is the one fact that you want the reader or viewer to understand most clearly about the poll?

2. Remember the wording of the questions. As you craft the story, keep in mind the wording of the questions. This is not to say you must repeat the question wording in the story. But the story must

be faithful to the wording. A question that found majority support for a five-day waiting period before an individual can purchase a handgun is not simply a question about gun control. It is about one type of gun control. Thus it would be wrong to say a majority of those questioned support gun control. You should write that a majority support a waiting period before an individual can buy a gun.

3. What's the second paragraph? This is not to say, literally, what is the second paragraph? The issue here is what is the "nut graf" of the story. This is the paragraph that tells the reader or the listener why he or she should care about this story, why the reporter and editor thought it was important enough to use. In the case of a poll story, does the poll show significant change? Do the poll results have an impact for legislation in Congress?

4. Get all the facts in. Remember to provide the reader or viewer all the facts needed to understand the poll results. It is a mistake to say that New Jersey Gov. Jim Florio has the support of 46 percent of those polled, while Republican Christine Whitman has the backing of 40 percent. You must provide remaining numbers: How many are undecided? How many would vote for other candidates? Giving half the results from a question is worse than giving none at all.

5. Add the technical details. Work into the story the basic information about the poll: how many people were interviewed, when the poll was done, who did it, who sponsored it, how it was done and the sampling error.

   Many of these facts can be worked in the various attribution phrases that are sprinkled through the story. For example, "Americans support a mutual reduction in nuclear weapons by the United States and the Soviet Union, according to a poll of 1,504 adults conducted Oct. 5–9." And a phrase such as "said the poll conducted by the Gallup Organization" can be tacked onto a sentence giving another poll number.

   Depending on style, another approach would be to craft a single paragraph that contains the technical details. Just make sure that it doesn't get cut in the editing process!

6. Don't try to pump too much into one story. One of the most confusing aspects of many poll stories comes when too many

results are crammed into one story. Just because you have the space or the time to cite the results from fifteen questions in a story doesn't mean you should. It is far better to pick out half a dozen items or fewer and explicate each one carefully. The other results can wait for another day and another story.

7. Don't use decimals In reporting poll numbers, you should always use whole percentages, never results with decimal points. Since these results are always subject to error, using decimals implies a precision that does not exist. The same goes for error margin figures.

GRAPHICS AND POLLS

Polls naturally lend themselves to graphic displays, both in print and in the broadcast media. The numbers that flow from the interviews make an excellent basis for pie charts, bar charts, line charts and many other graphic devices.

Polls fit in so well with graphics that there is often a temptation to make the graphic dramatic, even if the numbers don't really support the impression being left by the chart. In the 1960s and 1970s, a frequent offender was *U.S. News and World Report*, which often featured dramatic graphs that grossly overstated the data on which they were based.

Just as with headlines, the graphics based on a poll must accurately characterize the poll results. The graphic artist must work with the pollster or the reporter to understand the numbers and to portray them accurately. The substance of good graphic design in presenting information is beyond the scope of this book. But anyone seeking to understand the virtues and sins of graphic displays should turn to two works by Edward Tufte: *The Visual Display of Quantitative Information* (1983) and *Envisioning Information* (1990). Both are marvelous works that provide in prose and in design valuable lessons for anyone trying to make poll results understandable.

Now we turn to the powerful and important technique of putting the poll results in context and using other polls to add value to the results of a particular survey.

Chapter 15

REPORTING POLLS: NUMBERS IN CONTEXT

The Rev. Jesse Jackson, one of the great American political orators of the late twentieth century, came up with a retort during his 1984 presidential campaign to fire at critics he felt failed to understand the full meaning of his words.

"Text, without context, is pretext," Jackson liked to call out in the lustrous tones of a Baptist preacher.

Jackson's rhyming one-liner is just as true about polls as it is about political positions.

All public opinion surveys exist within a particular environment of time, place and information. After all, polls are simply repeatable, reliable and usually accurate measures of what people are thinking, saying and doing. To write about poll results without putting them into context can grossly distort the results.

This means that each report on a poll should take two matters into account in both the reporting and the analysis.

First, what is the news and information environment in which this poll was done? What events have occurred that may have shaped the public's level of knowledge and views? Many of the technical aspects of this were covered in Chapter 10 on the timing of polls.

There is one important caveat in this area. Just because a news event might have had an impact on public opinion, mere movement in the poll numbers does not, by itself, prove that the event shifted people's opinions. A well-designed poll can probe people's views to help provide support for an argument that the news events changed people's minds, but a simple shift in the numbers does not. In other words, coincidence is not causation.

In fact, any poll story with "because" in the lead probably needs a very careful second reading to make certain that the poll and the context of the poll support such a strong link of cause and effect.

Second, have any other polls ever been done on the same topic? Are there any recent polls on the same issue? Is there a history of asking questions on this topic? What does that trend show?

The comparison between polls taken on the same topic can provide some of the most useful and interesting poll stories on any topic. But it is not a simple matter of saying Poll A said this and now Poll B says that. Comparisons are often tricky.

ALL POLLS ARE NOT THE SAME!

Before going any further, one critical matter must be addressed. All polls are not done equally well. All poll results are not equally accurate.

In any comparison among polls, it is absolutely necessary to focus only on the polls that meet the basic standards laid out in this book.

It is a gross mistake to compare a professionally conducted, scientific state survey for a television station with a national poll done by volunteers for a special-interest group to push their political views. The state poll is probably quite valid: the national poll is not.

Unfortunately, this view can be taken too far—all the way to the Not Invented Here (NIH) syndrome. As mentioned earlier, many news organizations that conduct their own polls routinely ignore other surveys, particularly those done by other news organizations. After all, your newspaper or television station paid for this poll, so why shouldn't you push it? And why give a competitor any publicity for the poll it paid for?

This is a major error.

As we will explain throughout this chapter, results from multiple polls can often enhance the credibility and validity of a single given survey. Results from other polls can strengthen a poll story and can, indeed, provide the basis for excellent stories on change and contrast. Just because it is your poll, other surveys should not be ignored to the detriment of your readers and viewers.

USING POLLS OVER TIME

Whenever a poll comes across the journalist's desk, one of the earliest questions to be asked in the analysis of the results is this: Have there been any other polls done on this topic?

Comparing the latest poll's findings on a topic with previous polls provides two critical things to the journalist.

First, if the current poll has results on a number of questions that are quite similar to previous polls, you can have some increased confidence that the latest poll is valid. If the latest poll is wildly different, a red flag of warning shoots up. In a recent Louisiana Senate race, the available polls all indicated that the incumbent Democrat was going to win easily. Then a privately sponsored poll was released, showing the race was very tight. Because the results were so different from previous polls, the new poll was called into question and ultimately ignored. (The Democrat won in a landslide.)

Second, the comparison and contrast between the two polls can be very useful to the poll story. In fact, it may be the story.

The most obvious example of this is presidential job ratings. Whether President Clinton has a 60 percent excellent/good job rating from the public or a 45 percent rating is of only limited interest in and of itself. What is interesting is whether Clinton's job rating has changed. Are more people giving him high marks for his work as president—or fewer? After he sends more troops into Somalia, what does the public say about him?

Where did Clinton stand one year into his term compared with other presidents? (Answer, pretty low in the polls, about tied with where Ronald Reagan stood at the same time in his first term.)

Thus, the long trend lines from Gallup and Harris on presidential job ratings are interesting.

The political horse-race questions—matching one candidate against another—are another classic example where the contrast between two polls, the change that has occurred over time, is often the story.

One of the easiest stories to write about changing poll numbers is a story about the presidential job ratings. Usually, the writer is comparing presidential job ratings from two different polls conducted by the same organization using the same questions—only at different times. In this situation, there is usually no question of changes in survey methodology, question wording, sample base and the like that could distort the analysis of the changes in the poll results. (But a good reporter is always careful to check and make certain that there have been no methodological changes!)

It is more difficult to compare results from different questions from different polling firms, even on the same topic. Again, presidential job ratings are a good example.

The Gallup Poll uses a presidential job rating question that asks whether the respondent approves or disapproves of the job the president is doing. Then the respondent is asked if that stance is a strong approval (or disapproval) or not.

The Harris survey asks how the respondent would rate the president's work: excellent, good, only fair or poor. Then "excellent" is lumped with "good" and "only fair" with "poor" in reporting the results. The natural question would be whether Harris's "excellent/good" category is about the same as Gallup's "approve" category.

The answer is no: the two categories are different, and in some cases quite different.

Thus it is dangerous to compare the Gallup job rating with the Harris job rating and try to reach a conclusion about changes in the public view of the president. Don't do it.

Comparisons among polls conducted by different firms using different questions are sometimes necessary and useful. If a poll question has not been asked before, then there is no trend line on that question with which to compare it. A similar question on the same topic may, however, have been asked before and may provide a useful comparison to the latest poll. Whenever such a comparison is made, the differences in the question must be highlighted with an appropriate warning that the disparity in wording and methodology may be responsible for some of the variance in results.

Polls based on different populations can also be compared with very fruitful results.

For example, one might have a Texas state survey on school vouchers and the only other polls available on school vouchers are national. What good are they?

A great deal of good.

First, a national survey conducted by a reputable firm allows the state or local results to be put in a context bigger than a single poll would allow. For example, "Texans say they like the idea of the government providing vouchers that children could use at any school they please, a new Texas poll says. In fact, Texans like the idea a lot more than the country at large. While Texans say they favor vouchers by a 60–35 margin, a recent national poll said the county is split 48–45 on the topic."

USING TWO OR MORE POLLS TAKEN AT ABOUT THE SAME TIME

With the explosion of polling in America, journalists are often lucky enough to have more than one poll on the same subject conducted at about the same time. This abundance of riches (some might say excess) provides several opportunities to improve the reporting on public opinion. Additional polls provide much-needed context and confirmation of the poll's validity.

"It is a pollster's maxim that truth lies not in any single poll, but amid the preponderance of polls. Therefore, the sophisticated poll watcher benefits from examining several polls, looking for what the majority of them show and what they say in common," wrote *New York Times* pollster Michael R. Kagay in late 1993.

WHEN THEY AGREE

Does this poll have the same results as others done about the same time?

If the answer is yes, there is a greater confidence that the poll has some validity.

Part of the reason behind this increased confidence goes back to the statistics. Two different polls are based on independent samples. Thus the likelihood that both polls are flawed because of random variations in the sample (that is, the results diverge by more than the error margin from the true results) is far less than the probability that one poll suffers from that flaw.

In addition, two polls based on independent samples, conducted by independent organizations, using slightly different questions that still get roughly the same findings increase confidence in another important way. The agreement of the results from two professionally conducted polls means that all the methodological problems that can distort poll results are probably not present in this case. In other words, one poll tends to confirm the other.

WHEN THEY DISAGREE

But there are times when the polls do not agree. And that may be the story.

In 1980, the national polls on the presidential race varied substantially on the status of the contest between President Carter and Ronald Reagan. And none caught the big victory that Reagan eventually won that year.

The differences between the CBS News–*New York Times*, NBC News–Associated Press, ABC News–*Washington Post*, Gallup and Harris surveys were many. Many of the differences could not be easily explained.

But focusing on the technical details of the polls' disagreements turned out to miss the point. The point was that voters were not happy with the candidates, with the choice they faced and with the general state of the country. This unhappiness was reflected in the lack of stability in the poll findings on the Carter–Reagan matchup. Many of the pollsters (including one of the authors of this book) failed to emphasize this adequately.

After the election CBS News and *The New York Times* conducted a panel-back survey to see what happened among the voters they polled before Election Day. The results were a fascinating look at the complexity of voter choices when the people are not happy with the choice.

Whenever the polls disagree, the reporter needs to try to find out why.

The actual question wording must be examined side by side: Were there significant differences in the questions?

The timing of the interviewing must be inspected. Were the polls conducted at the same time? If not, did anything happen between the times the polls were conducted that could explain the difference?

Are the polls based on the same population? Are both samples of adults or of registered voters? Do both polls cover the same geographic areas—is one a statewide poll and one a regional survey?

The reporter needs to talk to the pollsters involved in cases of dueling polls to try to get their explanations for the differences. The pollsters will certainly defend their own work, but it is important to report their perspectives on the differences.

Even after long analysis, you may not be able to explain all the differences between polls. And that may be what the story says.

AVERAGING—LUMPING POLLS TOGETHER

A fairly recent development in dealing with the explosion of polling is to report all the polls on a given topic, especially on a political campaign. Then all the polls' results are averaged to give a set of summary numbers of "what the polls show." This technique builds directly on the virtue of each poll being an independent sample, thus providing increased confidence over a single poll's findings.

The averaging of poll results has the possible benefit of reducing the impact of any given poll, particularly any poll that differs significantly from the others. Averaging also tends to put a brake on the numbers' changing quickly. For the overall average to change quickly, all the polls would have to report new numbers and all of them would have to change.

This approach was used by *The New York Times* during the 1993 New York City mayor's race, where incumbent David Dinkins and Republican Rudy Giuliani were locked in a tight rematch of their 1989 fight. In the very tight race, the *Times's* averaging of poll results emphasized the closeness of the race and deemphasized the various polls that gave Dinkins or Giuliani any significant lead.

"The poll watcher should expect polls naturally to vary or disagree to some extent," the *Times's* pollster Michael Kagay wrote. "As a group polls should bracket or straddle the true value of what they are measuring—some a little high, some a little low, and some right on."

The potential problems with averaging arise from several factors. First, all the polls may not be of the same quality. Averaging a professionally conducted poll of 1,000 likely voters with a not-so-well-done poll of 300 adults is a mistake. One poll is probably more accurate than the other, but the average treats both the same.

Averaging can also mask changes in public opinion.

If the voters' views are changing, averaging the poll results will depress the reporting of the changes.

CONCLUSION

Public opinion surveys do not stand alone. Almost every poll can be understood more completely when other polls on the same or similar topics are used to highlight the important results and to give texture to the shape of opinion over time. The contrast between polls can often be more than just an addition to a news story—it may be the story.

Chapter 16

REPORTING POLLS: POLITICAL SURVEYS

Who is going to win the election?

Answering that question is at the heart of the romance between polls, politics and journalism. From this central question have come many of the innovations, the problems, the criticisms and the successes in all three fields.

The confluence of pressures in a democracy that periodically focus journalists, pollsters, politicians and the public on elections is enormous. Out of these pressures have come the major turning points in polling:

—The fiasco of the *Literary Digest* "poll" in 1936 was the impetus for the first great wave of news media polls from Gallup, Roper and Crossley.

—The 1948 poll disaster with "President Dewey" in the lead of the final horse-race polls on the race for the White House triggered major improvements in public polls.

—The great innovation of exit polls in the late 1960s came because the new medium of television had a consuming need to find out who had won as early as possible on Election Night and why they won. The Election Night broadcasts became the show-cases for the highly paid network anchors and the battlefields where bragging rights were won and lost by the network news divisions.

—For the first time in sixteen years, the presidential candidates held televised debates in 1976. The urge to know who had "won" the debates as quickly as possible triggered the development of instant polls from The Associated Press and others. These surveys sampled public opinion the moment the debate ended, allowing the next morning's newspapers to tell you what the public thought about the debate.

—The great flood of money into politics in the late 1970s and early 1980s gave rise to daily tracking polls, where the politicians or the news media took polls every day to get the quickest possible reading of the public's reaction to the day's events.

Handling political polls correctly is the hardest task facing the journalist writing about public opinion. Much of the public has come to resent polls as efforts to sway their personal political decisions, not just snapshots of the state of public opinion today. At least the two candidates' campaigns are watching every word carefully, ready to scream "bias" or "favoritism" at any time.

And, of course, political polls are the only truly visible polls that can be proven right or wrong on Election Day. Either the poll had the right candidate in the lead before the election, or it did not. Nobody can "prove" a poll is right or wrong on a president's job rating. But the political polls face that exact test every Election Day.

HORSE-RACE POLLS

Most of the attention on the political polls is focused on the so-called horse-race questions. These are the queries that simulate the election decision and thus tease out of the potential voters who they will cast their ballots for in the election to come. The question usually goes something like "If the election were held today, would you vote for Bill Clinton, the Democrat; George Bush, the Republican; or Ross Perot, the independent?"

This is just one question out of many on a political poll. Does it deserve the attention it gets? No. Will that ever change? No, not as long as elections have at least a winner and a loser.

The horse-race question is designed to answer one question directly and one indirectly. First, who is leading in the race for president, or senator, or governor right now? Second, have the candidates' standings changed since the last poll?

So how do you analyze a horse-race question to decide which candidate is leading? That's simple, one might say: The leading candidate is the one with the biggest number beside his or her name in the poll results, right? Not exactly.

The leading candidate in a poll is the one whose lead in the results over the nearest challenger is statistically significant. That is, the leader has to be ahead by a large enough margin that the lead is probably not just the result of sampling error.

In late March 1992, *The Los Angeles Times* conducted a national survey that said President Bush had the backing of 48 percent of the adults interviewed, while Bill Clinton had the support of 46 percent, with the rest undecided.

This poll did not say, show, find or demonstrate that Bush was ahead of Clinton in the race for the White House. The poll results can only be called a "dead heat," a "statistical tie," a "close race" or "too close to call."

Why? Because this poll, with a sample of about 1,000 adults, had a sampling error of about plus or minus three percentage points. As discussed in the chapter on sampling error, this means that chance variations in the sample could mean that the "real" level of Bush's support was as low as 45 percent or as high as 51 percent. For the same reason, Clinton's support could be as low as 43 percent or as high as 49 percent. Thus, given the potential impact of sampling error, the true levels of public opinion in the presidential race could be a big Bush margin of 51–43, or a Clinton edge of 49–45. The possibility that either 51–43 or 49–45 is correct, however, is very, very, very small. The most likely "true" reading is 48–46.

Given this uncertainty, it is flat wrong to say Bush is leading. And that demonstrates the first commandment of horse-race polls:

If the margin between the candidates is less than the sampling error for the poll, neither candidate is leading in the race. The contest can only be called a close one.

This is one of the hardest rules for all journalists—from headline writers to television anchors—to live by. There is an often overwhelming urge to declare one candidate the leader. It is simple, it is easy, it is clear and it makes for a good story. Saying the race is "too close to call" is complicated and requires substantial caveats and explanation. But the complicated story is the correct one in this case. To do otherwise is just wrong.

Later in 1992, NBC News and *The Wall Street Journal* reported on a September poll that gave Clinton 51 percent and Bush 41 percent among 1,506 registered voters. So is Clinton leading in this poll? Absolutely, according to the second commandment of horse-race polls.

If the margin between the candidates is greater than twice the sampling error for the poll, then the candidate with the greatest level of support is leading.

Why is this so?

The NBC/*Wall Street Journal* poll gave Clinton a 51–41 edge, with a three percentage point sampling error. That means that sampling error alone could push Clinton's standing as high as 54 or as low as 48. For Bush, the results could range from 44 to 38. To use the same analysis as before, the true standings could vary from a 54-38 Clinton lead to a 48–44 Clinton lead.

Thus, even if sampling error inflicted its harshest penalty on the results, the real standings would still put Clinton in the lead.

Actually, the statistics that lie behind this rule are more complicated than this description would indicate. The statistical analysis would actually allow a bit more flexibility in these races. But this rule is a conservative one that has worked well in practice.

There is still one more situation that needs to be addressed.

In late October 1992, CBS and *The New York Times* conducted a poll that put the presidential race this way:

Clinton	42 percent
Bush	37 percent
Perot	17 percent

With a sample of 1,369 likely voters and a sampling error of three percentage points, what does this poll show? The Clinton–Bush margin is not less than three percentage points, so the race is not a "dead heat." The margin is not more than six percentage points either, so Clinton is not clearly leading.

In this gray area, the journalist's task is quite tricky.

A careful statistical analysis of this situation would show that the probabilities favor a Clinton lead, but there remains a relatively small possibility that Bush is actually ahead.

To handle this situation, the stories and the analyses of the poll must include a variety of carefully crafted caveats and qualifiers to give the readers and the viewers an accurate picture without involving them in the statistics. Useful phrases include saying Clinton has a slight lead, a narrow margin, a slim advantage, a small lead. It is still a close race, but it isn't too close to call. And that is the third commandment of horse-race polls:

If the difference between two candidates' levels of support is more than the sampling error margin, but less than twice the sampling error, then the candidate with the greatest support can be said to have a small lead in the race. But the closeness of the contest must be emphasized and careful qualifiers added to describe the situation accurately.

SPINNING THE POLLS

The political campaign managers and consultants will always try to put the best light on poll results for their candidate. A poll showing their candidate far behind the incumbent will be described as showing the incumbent's weaknesses. A poll putting their candidate ahead by two points will be trumpeted as a lead.

All of this is just another variation on "spinning the story" for the journalists, as the political professionals try to put the best "spin" on the facts to help their candidate. Good, professional consultants will not lie, but they will highlight the positives and downplay the negatives.

"Campaigns do not hesitate to ignore the strictures of sampling error when claiming they are ahead. Campaigns that find themselves trailing another candidate by less than the margin of error, however, are suddenly blessed with great statistical insight and claim that the polls show the two candidates 'even,' " writes poll-ster Harrison Hickman (Mann and Orren 1992: 122).

A good journalist will listen to what the campaigns have to say, of course. But a good journalist can use the tools described in this book to avoid accepting the campaign's spin on the numbers.

POLL MARGINS

It should be said that the margin one candidate has over another in a poll is grossly overemphasized. Not only are the margins subject to greater variance than a single poll number, but they tend to exaggerate the situation by their very nature.

When analyzing a horse-race poll, it is important to look at signposts other than just the margin.

For example, if the incumbent candidate is below the 50 percent mark in a poll on a two-way race, the incumbent may be facing some trouble. What such a poll says is that a majority of the potential voters aren't saying they will back the candidate for reelection. This is an indication that a challenger may be able to exploit the public's lack of satisfaction with the incumbent.

How many people are undecided about the choice? This may be an indicator of big trouble for the candidate who is apparently leading.

The demographics of candidates' supporters are always useful. Is the candidate capturing the lion's share of his or her party's adherents in a general election? Are the independents breaking for one candidate or the other? Is there a pattern of support among various racial groups or in geographic areas that is significant?

"COULD BE GOOD, COULD BE BAD, TOO SOON
TO TELL"

In June 1988, Massachusetts Gov. Michael Dukakis held a big lead over Vice President George Bush in the horse-race polls on the presidential race. At least one poll put his margin at seventeen percentage points.

Bush had been campaigning hard, but the momentum that Dukakis had built up with a string of Democratic primary victories was carrying him along through the early summer. There was much discussion of the Martin Van Buren factor (the last vice president to be elected to the presidency while vice president), the weaknesses in the Republican Party after eight years of control of the White House, and so on.

In November 1988, it was President-elect Bush, not President-elect Dukakis. What happened? Were the polls wrong?

What happened was very simple: a presidential campaign happened. Nearly six months of speeches, television ads, debates and news coverage took place between the June polls and the November vote. And it should not have surprised anyone that the campaign had an impact.

One could argue that Dukakis was never really seventeen points ahead of Bush, that the poll numbers were influenced by abnormal factors. What was clear from many polls in May and June 1988 was that Dukakis was ahead of Bush in the voters' sentiments, substantially ahead by some measures.

But none of the polls of June tell you what is going to happen in the voting booths in November. More than $100 million is spent in a modern presidential campaign to try to change voters' choices—and that has an impact.

The point is that people's attitudes can and do change over time, changes that can easily reverse the outcome of an election. Polls months from an election are interesting, they are useful, but they don't tell you who will win.

Roy Wetzel, longtime head of the NBC News election unit, likes to describe horse-race questions months before an election with an analogy. How many people know what kind of salad dressing they will choose for a Thursday night dinner six months from now? Some do: they always have the same dressing. But, for most of us, the question taps our habits, our inclinations, our past behavior: all of which may, or may not, determine what kind of salad dressing we have six months hence.

Likewise, some voters will always vote Democratic, or always vote Republican. But there is a substantial portion of the electorate that is not that tightly committed to a political party and that makes its choices after a great deal of information is provided through the campaigns and the news media. It is these voters who can and will change their minds about the presidential candidates, perhaps several times, before actually pulling the lever for one contender.

WHO VOTES?

Only slender majorities of American adults actually take the trouble to vote in the presidential race every four years. And some state primary elections are decided by fewer than 25 percent of the registered voters.

Given this sad fact of American political participation, preelection polls face the difficult task of figuring out which adults are likely to vote and providing poll results that accurately reflect the opinions of the likely voters. All pollsters have their own, sometimes proprietary, method for identifying people who are most likely to vote. Some call the people selected "likely voters," while others use the term "probable electorate." Whatever the phrase, the goal is to accurately identify those people who will most probably vote.

Just asking someone if he or she is going to vote turns out to be a very poor indicator of actual voting intention. Many Americans feel a civic duty to vote, even if they never do so. Thus, when asked about voting, they routinely say they fully intend to cast their ballot. Some of those people will never get near the polling booth.

The task is also complicated by the patchwork quilt of U.S. voting rules. Each state sets its own rules for who qualifies to vote and how one can exercise that right. In most states, Americans must take two steps to vote. First, they must register to vote, usually at least a month before the election. Second, they must go to the polls and vote. (In many other democratic countries, all citizens are automatically registered to vote.)

Although new federal rules on voter registration were passed in the early 1990s, there is still a substantial variance in the laws from state to state.

Thus, the first method to identify those who will vote is to ask if the respondent is registered to vote. There is some tendency of Americans to claim they are registered when they are not—again the aura of civic duty—but this overstatement seems to be less than that about voting itself.

The caveat here is time. The longer before the election this question is asked, the less valuable it is, particularly if there are major efforts under way to register new voters. Since a citizen can register up to fifteen or thirty days before the election, asking whether someone is registered to vote eight months before the election is not a completely pure measurement.

Faced with low turnout and widely varying state laws, pollsters depend on a series of questions about a person's past behavior and current interest in politics to screen out people who are not likely to vote. For example, people who voted in the last presidential election are far more likely to vote than not to vote in the next election. Citizens who say they are following news about the election campaign very closely are far more likely voters than those who say they are paying little attention to the campaign.

The pollsters then use the answers to several questions—including "Are you registered to vote?"—to screen the sample down to likely voters only. Various statistical methods are used, from creating an index of the answers to weighting each respondent's answers by the calculated probability of voting.

The result of all the statistics and computer time is poll numbers based on opinions of those most likely to actually vote, not on the answers from the whole sample. This likely voter sample is smaller than the overall sample, and has a higher sampling error margin.

Does all this work to create a subsample of likely voters make a difference in the numbers?

Usually it does, and usually the impact is not great.

Likely voters, for example, tend to be older and more educated on average than all adults. This can mean that likely voters are slightly more Republican than the full sample.

Typically, political polls are focused on samples of registered voters or of all adults. As the election draws closer, the pollsters begin to release results focused on likely voters to match the Election Day circumstances more closely.

Occasionally, the switch from registered voters to likely voters in poll reporting itself is news.

In 1992, the Gallup Organization conducted daily tracking polls for *USA Today* and the Cable News Network (CNN) in the closing weeks of the presidential campaign. Tracking polls are a quite specialized type of survey in which complete samples of respondents are interviewed each night. The nightly samples are then added together—sometimes two nights' interviewing, sometimes three nights'—to provide the poll results. Tracking polls face major methodological problems, but they do allow pollsters, politicians and the news media to see changes among the voters quickly.

The Gallup/*USA Today*/CNN polls were based on registered voters for much of the month of October and showed some substantial Clinton margins. The Democrat's lead was as much as eighteen percentage points as late as the two-day tracking poll completed before the third presidential debate on October 19. Clinton was the choice of 48 percent, to 30 percent for Bush and 15 percent for Perot among 1,000 registered voters.

After the third debate, it was clear that the race began to tighten. Other polls, including tracking surveys done by ABC News, showed that Clinton's lead was eroding.

(Such tightening in the final weeks of a campaign is quite common. Voters begin to focus on the race, make firmer and firmer choices. Particularly when the incumbent is trailing in the final weeks, the margin tends to be reduced.)

Then, on October 26, the pollster and the two news organizations shifted from the registered voter base to the likely voter base. The shift was long planned. Both CNN and *USA Today* explained the change and gave horse-race results using both population bases.

Despite all the caveats, the impact of the change was to make the race look much tighter. The October 24–25 poll of registered voters gave Clinton a 42–31 lead. The October 25–26 poll based on likely voters made it 42–36. An eleven-point margin seemed to drop to six points overnight.

"It was an unfortunate coincidence that we began reporting results for likely voters as the race narrowed dramatically," the authors of the poll said after the election.

Three days later, October 28–29, the Gallup/*USA Today*/CNN tracking poll was showing 41 percent Clinton, 40 percent Bush, based on likely voters.

Was Bush on the verge of winning reelection with a dramatic last-minute surge? The news stories focused on the surge and the possible reasons for it. The numbers certainly suggested it was possible. The ABC News tracking poll showed the race tightening, but never to the degree of the other survey (Rosentiel 1993:327–331).

In any case, the surge in the poll numbers evaporated and Clinton went on to win by more than five percentage points.

The issue of registered voters versus likely voters certainly can make a difference, as the 1992 experience attests. And it suggests that shifts to a likely voter base should occur ahead of Election Day, when there is more time for the news media—and the public—to absorb the impact of any changes that come from methodological moves by the pollsters.

TRACKING POLLS

Tracking polls are quite useful, if quite limited, tools for monitoring the dynamics of a political campaign. They can detect swings in public opinion as a result of events: that is why campaigns use tracking polls as a tactical tool to try to detect which strategies are working and which are not.

The lure of tracking polls for the news media is undeniable. There are new poll numbers each and every day. The march of the numbers across the calendar makes for excellent graphics in print and on television in an era when graphics are hot.

But tracking polls have their drawbacks. The principal one is that the pollster is not able to repeatedly call potential respondents who are not available on the first try by the interviewer. Academic studies show that hard-to-reach respondents are different from those typically interviewed on the first call and that the differences can be significant in political polls.

Given the pressure to complete at least several hundred interviews per night, tracking polls use shorter questionnaires than other types of political polls. This means less depth in the questions and the topics covered, and an increased focus on the horse race.

With tracking polls more and more commonplace, the political campaigns are turning even negative poll numbers to their advantage. Bill Clinton captured a rhetorical victory in the 1992 New Hampshire Democratic presidential primary—even though he lost. Clinton labeled himself the "Comeback Kid" on the basis of his 26 percent of the vote, which was more than the 19 or 20 percent that he had been getting in the tracking polls. Clinton lost to Paul Tsongas, who received 35 percent of the vote. But the "Comeback

Kid" tag stuck and helped Clinton look like a winner even when he lost. E. J. Dionne of *The Washington Post* calls this the "tracking poll effect" (Mann and Orren 1992:165).

"I CAN'T MAKE UP MY MIND"

Every poll on a political contest finds some people who say they are truly undecided, they have not made up their minds which candidate they are going to back.

Some polls ask which candidate a respondent is "leaning" toward. Other pollsters instruct their interviewers to push the respondents forcefully to elicit a choice.

No matter which method is used, there are still always some undecided likely voters.

But there are no undecided voters on Election Day. A citizen votes for either one candidate or the other—or does not vote.

Thus, the pollster must decide what to do about that usually small number of undecideds in the poll results as Election Day approaches.

One approach has been to discard the undecided and recompute the percentages based on those who have made up their minds. This assumes either that the undecided don't vote or that they will split their votes as the more committed voters do. Both are somewhat chancy propositions.

Another approach has been to allocate the undecided voters on the basis of one or more characteristics. For example, Democratic undecided voters might be allocated to the Democratic candidate, and Republican undecideds to the Republican contender.

The problem with this approach is that it assumes the undecided voters will "come home" to vote as others like them will. That may be true, but it is again problematical.

An approach suggested by Nick Panagakis of Market Shares Corp. says that undecided voters usually decide in favor of the challengers. His theory is that voters are not undecided between the candidates, but undecided about the incumbent. Since the incumbent is typically the best-known candidate, this implies that voters who are undecided about a candidate they know much about will end up voting against that candidate.

The Gallup Poll used the Panagakis approach on its final preelection poll of 1992, allocating five of the six percentage points of undecideds to Clinton. That gave the final Gallup numbers as 49 percent Clinton, 37 percent Bush and 14 percent Perot. Unfortunately for Gallup, the unadjusted numbers were closer for Clinton than the adjusted ones. The final election returns were 43–38–19.

The weaknesses in many methods that allocate the undecided votes is that they are not firmly based on theory and tested in practice.

Rather than using a rigid, mechanical approach to dealing with the undecided numbers, a more reasonable approach is to use the undecideds as a warning flag. The undecided voter is a wild card in many elections. Particularly with an incumbent in the race, a substantial undecided bloc in the polls often indicates unhappiness with the incumbent and perhaps trouble on Election Day.

IT'S ALL OVER, OR "WILL YOU STILL LOVE ME TOMORROW?"

It's close to Election Day, the candidate's lead over his or her opponent is large and the likely voters seem certain. It's all over, right?

No.

In May 1978, The Associated Press and NBC News conducted a preprimary poll in New Jersey in advance of that state's June voting. Incumbent Republican Sen. Clifford Case faced a little-known economist named Jeff Bell in his party's primary.

The AP-NBC News poll gave Case a 68–19 lead over Bell among likely Republican voters. So it was all over.

But nobody told the Republican voters. Bell beat Case narrowly that June, in one of the biggest primary upsets of the year. (Bell's electoral string was ended that fall by a Democrat named Bill Bradley, late of the New York Knicks of the National Basketball Association, who won the Senate seat.)

Bell won because GOP primary turnout was astonishingly low. Fewer than 250,000 votes were cast in the primary, and Case was retired by the voters after twenty-four years in the Senate.

A poll taken closer to the primary might have picked up the trouble for Case. A more in-depth analysis might have exposed the weaknesses in the incumbent's support.

Whatever the exact reason in this case, large margins in preelection polls never guarantee anyone victory. Only the votes that are cast on election day can do that.

CRITICISM OF HORSE-RACE POLLS

The journalistic focus on horse-race polls is much criticized—by academicians, columnists, the public and even the media. And much of the criticism has a valid point: where concentration on who's ahead drowns out information about the candidate's stands on the issues, the candidate's performance and the substantive contrasts between the contenders, the journalism suffers and so do the voters seeking to make a rational choice.

The proliferation of polls, particularly those sponsored by the media, has provided more material for horse-race journalism. With the news media funding the polls, there is more and more pressure to use the numbers. And that has some very negative effects.

"It is a rare reporter, indeed, who does not treat his or her poll story as a journalistic Holy Grail that explains the sum and substance of a campaign and its candidates," pollster Harrison Hickman says (Mann and Orren 1992:101).

It is beyond the scope of this book to discuss the full range of campaign coverage, the good and the bad, by print and broadcast outlets, because this book is focused on polls. But polls should not be the centerpiece of campaign coverage. The candidates, the issues and the government the politicians seek to lead should be the focus. The recent efforts—such as by David Broder of *The Washington Post* and by *The Charlotte Observer* in North Carolina and *The Wichita Eagle* in Kansas—to keep the focus on the substance of the choices facing the voters are a welcome change that will spread to other cities and other news outlets in the years to come.

Chapter 17

REPORTING POLLS: EXIT POLLS AND PROJECTIONS

The polls have just closed in thirteen states in the East, and it looks like the Democrats are doing very, very well. We are now projecting that Democrats will hold onto the Senate seats they have in Georgia, Tennessee and Alabama while knocking off Republican incumbents in four other states.

It's only 8 P.M. eastern time on Election Night, and each of the major television network news anchors is able to tell viewers who won the races in many states and why they won. Using language something like the paragraph above, the news anchors perform what appears to be nothing short of magic: announcing who has won an election before the first vote is tabulated.

That magic is made possible by one of the major innovations in polling in the last three decades: the exit poll, interviewing voters as they actually leave the precincts, tallying the questionnaires and making public the results sometime later on Election Day.

Exit polls were invented by the American television networks to feed their need for as much election information as possible, as early as possible, as the voters cast their ballots.

The logistics of these polls are awesome. A national exit poll may involve more than 1,000 interviewers at precincts across the country, obtaining filled-out questionnaires from more than 40,000 voters. Several hundred data entry clerks in huge computer centers transcribe the data from the questionnaires as the interviewers read it to them over the telephone. The data are punched into the computer and made instantly available to the television networks and the others who support the effort.

HISTORY OF EXIT POLLS

Asking voters who they cast their ballots for has long been a common occurrence on Election Day in America. At least since the late nineteenth century—when the secret ballot was introduced in American elections—political machines worked hard to ensure that the right people voted and the people voted right.

Today, voters in key elections across the country are asked who they voted for, but for a much different reason than in the past. Now it is the news media asking the questions, not the political bosses. In fact, the political bosses now get much of their Election Day information from the news media.

The exit polls are a very recent phenomenon. During the last thirty years, exit polls have grown from experiment to the single most visible part of election coverage on television and in newspapers.

The birth of the exit poll is a topic entangled in controversy. In 1964, NBC News conducted an experiment in vote counting using rudimentary exit poll techniques in the June 2 California primary. Only ten precincts were covered, and what data analysis there was came from some adding machines (Lavrakas and Holley 1991:64, 89). I. A. "Bud" Lewis, later director of the NBC News election unit, claimed that this was the first exit poll (Lavrakas and Holley 1991:64).

In the 1967 Kentucky gubernatorial election, CBS News conducted what Warren Mitofsky says is the first true exit poll. The results were used to assist in making a projection of the outcome. Actual vote results were a key part of the analysis (Lavrakas and Holley 1991:88).

From these early efforts in the late 1960s, exit polls were used to analyze the election returns, to help provide information on why the winner came out on top.

Before the advent of exit polls, the television networks and others used specially selected precincts to estimate how specific groups voted. For example, precincts in heavily black areas were used to estimate the voting behavior of black voters. Similarly, precincts in heavily ethnic areas, in areas of high and low income and in areas where specific religions were concentrated provided the results used in on-the-air analysis of how groups of voters voted.

All of these early forms of vote analysis were subject to possibly extreme bias. First, few precincts are composed entirely of voters from a single group. Second, those who live in homogeneous precincts are not necessarily indicative of those in the same group who live in more heterogeneous areas. Finally, many of the most interesting groups such as age groups and new voters, almost never are concentrated in ways that can be measured using this type of information.

So the primitive analysis techniques of using precinct results did not and could not produce truly accurate information. They added interest to the election analysis, but it was subject to substantial error.

Exit polls, however, do not suffer from any of these problems. While they have other difficulties, such as response rates, they are not limited to geographically based analysis.

The use of exit polls has provided a wealth of information about who voted and why they voted as they did. In addition, because of the size of the samples, analysis is possible on groups who would normally not be represented in a poll in sufficient numbers.

HOW IT IS DONE

The exit poll is a special version of the intercept poll, in which people who have just voted are asked to complete questionnaires as they leave the polling place. There are two main purposes for this type of poll: projections of elections and analysis of results.

The exit poll is conducted in a sample of precincts within the jurisdiction in question. For example, a sample of precincts may be drawn from a city, a state or a congressional district. These samples are normally systematic samples of voters, where the precincts are drawn in such a way that each registered voter has a known chance of selection.

It is important to note that drawing a sample of precincts where each precinct has an equal chance of selection is normally not a valid sampling technique. This is because there is often a systematic bias in precinct sizes; quite often urban precincts are much larger in terms of numbers of voters than are rural precincts. As a result, a random sample of precincts will oversample areas that have smaller precincts.

In many cases, special sampling techniques are used to insure against certain random fluctuations in precinct selection. This process, called stratification, divides the jurisdiction into various groups, called strata, which are then sampled in appropriate numbers. These strata may be geographic, such as the southern part of the state, or they may be based upon voters' behavior, such as the percent who voted for the Democratic candidate in the last election. By choosing a characteristic that will be important in the election, the chance that a heavily biased sample will be chosen is greatly reduced.

Once the sample is chosen, interviewers are recruited for each sample precinct. Questionnaires are then printed and distributed to the interviewers. Each interviewer is assigned a precinct location, specific interviewing hours and times to call in results to a central location.

At each precinct, the interviewer counts the voters leaving the polling place and selects respondents on the basis of a predetermined interval—such as every fifth voter or every tenth voter. The voter selected at this interval is approached and asked to participate in the survey. The voter is handed a questionnaire on a clipboard along with a pencil or pen and is asked to complete the instrument, fold it and place it in a ballot box or large envelope.

The length of the questionnaire varies according to its use. Where it is designed only as a projection tool, the exit poll instrument is very short: a question on voting for each office and some demographic questions. Where analysis is the goal, the questionnaire may contain thirty or more questions.

In some cases, the interviewer also collects information on voters who refuse to complete the questionnaire. Observations of age, race and sex are collected for potential analysis of nonresponse bias. This can be extremely important where differential refusal rates among groups can significantly bias the sample. For example, if candidate A is very strong among the elderly and if many more elderly refuse to complete the questionnaires, the exit poll might seriously underestimate the strength of the candidate. Weighting to correct for such refusals can provide a guide to the potential nonresponse bias in the survey.

At the end of each interviewing period, the interviewer takes the completed questionnaires to a telephone and dials the central collection point. There, a data entry operator enters the information that identifies the precinct and the results of each questionnaire.

The information collected is processed immediately and made available for analysis in a very short time. If the goal is analysis, the results are then prepared for presentation either on the air or in print. If the goal is projection, the results are entered into a statistical model of the election that then provides information which may allow the projection of a winner in the race.

The reporters or producers seeking to use the exit poll material usually have terminals connected directly to the computer containing the exit poll data. Thus, the journalists can call up numbers based on the most recent data and examine them for nuggets to be used in the Election Night broadcast or in newspaper stories explaining the election.

EXIT POLL JOURNALISM

Turning exit poll material into a news story is a special case that highlights the clash of values between journalism and survey research.

A reporter or producer writing an exit poll story must start and complete the poll analysis very quickly. Depending on the access to the data and when the story is needed, the journalist may have anywhere from several hours to several minutes to analyze the data and turn them into a news story. That story may only be a paragraph for the television anchor to read on the air. For example, a candidate may have just claimed that the Hispanic vote was the key to his victory. With an exit poll available, the producer could quickly craft a sentence or two on what the exit poll shows on the Hispanic vote.

Writing an exit poll story is not that different from writing any poll story for print or broadcast. Of course, when the media outlet has sponsored the exit poll, the journalist already knows the key facts of poll sponsorship, sample size and design, question wording and the like.

Faced with an exit poll, the first step a journalist should take is to examine the internal numbers in the poll to make certain they are reasonable. Given the speed with which exit polls are done, all the potential problems of respondent selection, refusal rates and data entry errors are quite real.

To help in this first step, as well as in later analysis, a well-prepared journalist will have the results of previous exit polls on the desk when analyzing the latest numbers, so that historical comparisons can be made if appropriate. The results of the late preelection polls should also be available, since they can provide comparison and contrast to the actual results.

The journalist first looks at the demographics of the voters to see if any numbers are substantially different from past years. For example, African-American voters made up only about 8 percent of the New Jersey voters in the 1993 gubernatorial election, down from 12 percent in the 1989 race. This difference was real, not an artifact of a poll problem. But it is these types of differences that a journalist looks for, first to make certain that the sample is not wildly out of sync and then to determine the makeup of the winner's backers.

PROJECTIONS

Exit polls are the key to one of the most controversial aspects of modern public opinion polling: the sophisticated ability to determine quickly which candidate has won a race, particularly when the race is not close.

With the development of network television election units came the first modern exit polls, as mentioned above, on the Kentucky governor's race in 1967. These network election units also sought to improve the ability to decide who the winner was in an election, which the networks called an election projection. These projection efforts sought to use statistical models of the vote to allow quick declarations of winners in races of interest.

The projection models developed in the late 1960s and 1970s relied on much of the same statistical bedrock as polls. One such model relies on drawing a sample of precincts in a state, for example, and then trying to quickly obtain the votes from those precincts on Election Night. This approach—sometimes called key precinct models—uses the same stratification techniques as mentioned in the design of exit polls.

But the projection models have additional data with which to work: the voting history of the precincts involved. The past votes in the sample precincts are collected and put into the computer well in advance of Election Night. As the votes from the current election are input on election night, the model analyzes the present vote against the historical vote to help determine the winner.

Precinct models are quite fast, where the precinct-level vote can be obtained. But more and more counties are using vote technologies that preclude a precinct-level count. In addition, precinct models involve sampling and other potential sources of error, making it difficult to call the winner in close races.

For close races, county-level projection models have been developed. These statistical models use the raw vote from every county in a state as it comes in and compare it with the historical vote in the county—just as the precinct model does for the key precincts. By analyzing the current county vote versus history, a determination of the winner can often be made. But county vote tallies come in much more slowly than precinct tallies, meaning it can be hours after the polls close that a projection can be made.

Exit polls can speed up the election projection process even more.

But exit polls were not used as the sole basis for projecting elections for many years. It wasn't until the early 1980s that exit polls were used as the basis for calling elections. NBC News called Ronald Reagan the winner of the presidency at 8:15 P.M. eastern time in 1980, using exit polls and key precincts to project Reagan as the winner in enough states where the polls had closed. For CBS, the first time exit poll results were used as the sole basis for calling an election was in the New Jersey governor's race in 1981. And CBS called Jim Florio the winner. Unfortunately, that was incorrect. Florio lost narrowly to Tom Kean (*Editor and Publisher* 1981:27).

Using an exit poll and the vote history from the precincts in which the poll is conducted, it is possible to determine which candidate has won a race fairly early, usually by the time the polls close in a state. If the winner's margin is large enough to overwhelm the potential sources of error in the exit poll, then the election projection can be made at poll close, if not before.

THE EXIT POLL/PROJECTION DILEMMA

Once exit polls provided the data that revealed who won an election before the votes were counted, journalists were faced with a serious dilemma. Should the results of the exit poll, including the winner of a race, be reported even if the voters are still casting their ballots in that race?

The general answer to this question has been no. In testimony before congressional committees, representatives of the networks have repeatedly promised not to "call" or project an election prior to the close of the polls. In addition, there have been promises not to even "characterize" an election, that is, to describe one candidate as having a commanding lead or make other descriptive statements about the results.

This is really not that different from the journalistic practice of adhering to an embargo on a story until the embargo is lifted. The major difference is that journalists have discovered the information on their own.

This dilemma is even more of a problem in a presidential election. The U.S. Constitution provides the election of a president by a series of state elections that technically elect persons called electors, who meet and actually vote for president. As a result of the winner-take-all system and the electoral college structure, a candidate wins the presidency by winning a simple majority of the electoral votes. Because these votes are distributed in the same way that congressional representation is, the majority of the electoral votes are in the eastern half of the country.

When a presidential candidate wins by a significant margin, the results in states in the Eastern and Central time zones are often sufficient to give him or her the election.

Prior to projection systems, the time it took to collect the vote meant that the winners were not known until late on Election Night or the next day.

With modern projection systems and exit polls, it is possible to determine with reasonable certainty the winner in a one-sided race prior to the close of the polls. If a group adheres to the "projection only after the polls have closed" doctrine, it is still possible, and in fact likely, that the total states projected for a candidate may exceed the required majority of the electoral college well before the polls have closed in the Mountain and Pacific time zones. In 1980, NBC projected Reagan the winner at 8:15 P.M. Eastern time, more than two and a half hours prior to the close of the polls in the West. CBS and ABC followed, using projection models, and called the race before the polls had closed on the West Coast.

While there has been a great deal of controversy over this type of projection, the research on the impact of the projections on the vote in the West is inconclusive (Lavrakas and Holley 1991:89–93). Still, many voters express concern that their vote doesn't seem to count if the winner is known before their state is even considered.

That is absolutely true. In fact, politicians have structured campaigns on the basis of their understanding of the electoral college system. A candidate does not have to do well in all states to win; rather, he or she only needs to win enough states to get a majority of the electoral college. Candidates schedule time and campaign advertising to win key states rather than to attempt to win all states.

There have been several proposals to eliminate this problem. The first, and most likely, is a common poll closing time across the country. While this might burden the people who work in the voting booth, the proposal has a great deal of support from those who oppose early projections. This proposal could be implemented by the adoption of a federal law, since the federal government has the ability to set the conditions of a federal election.

The second proposal, which would have far-reaching consequences, is to provide for the election of the president by popular vote, not electoral vote. In that case, the polls would not be closed until the last voter had voted, and early projections would be impossible. This proposal would require a constitutional amendment.

EXIT POLLS IN THE 1990s

As a method to reduce costs, the networks, including CNN, formed a cooperative venture in 1990 to provide exit polls and projections instead of competing with each other. This group, called

Voter Research and Surveys (VRS), provides projections to the members as well as raw poll data for analysis. The members, each of whom saves many millions of dollars by participating, made the news judgments on when to report the projections and how to analyze the exit poll results.

In late 1993, VRS and the News Election Service, which tabulates top-of-the-tickets votes for the networks and The Associated Press, were merged.

A number of observers have expressed concern over this combination. The issue seems to be a lack of competitive sources for exit poll results and projections. Clearly, without competing systems, it is more likely that a projection error could be made and accepted by the media. Fortunately, the accuracy record of projections by the national media is excellent. It is also possible that a failure of the projection system, a computer problem or a natural disaster could deprive the American public of instant results on Election Night. While this would certainly be a disappointment, there should be no lingering result other than increased calls for competitive projection systems.

The arguments for multiple exit polls, however, are more compelling. With only a single questionnaire, even if the sample is properly executed, the results will include only those topics chosen by the media pool. Important issues may be ignored because they cannot command the attention of a majority of the pool members. The use of a single questionnaire means that fewer questions can be asked.

A number of options have been used to minimize this problem. For example, each member of the pool in 1992 was allowed to include some private questions that were not supported by others, so that topics which did not command a majority did get included. The lack of space in the questionnaire was addressed by conducting multiple national exit polls for the pool. Clearly, while fewer questions were included, the limits were not nearly as severe as initially argued.

Perhaps the most serious problem is the lack of any information with which to compare the results of the exit poll. Prior to VRS, multiple national exit polls were conducted by the networks. After the election, the results of most of these were made available for academic research. This allowed for the comparison of the exit polls and the determination of systematic differences between them. With only a single national poll, this lack of comparative information could lead to erroneous conclusions. In 1992, *The Los Angeles Times* conducted a national exit poll. This provided some comparative information that was useful. In the future, if no other national exit polls are conducted, the media will be vulnerable to problems in the poll.

Chapter 18

THE FUTURE

As you wake in the morning, your Personal Information Assistant (PIA) clicks on with one of the 500 channels automatically selected on the basis of the choices you made at the start of the week. Part of the morning routine for the PIA is to pose a series of questions to you on the major public policy issue of the day. The answers you give as you eat breakfast—plus those from thousands of others—are automatically tabulated and presented to your congressional representatives who have to vote on the issue later that day.

As a working journalist, your digital communicator that long ago replaced the wrist watch provides you with up-to-date information on the national polling being conducted. As you interview a member of the congressional leadership, you can get the latest figures on public opinion, as of that moment. Whether you are in broadcast or print, all the information you have gathered—in words, sound and pictures—is immediately available across the country to those who switch to your channel.

THE OPINION TRIANGLE

This high-technology view of the future may be on the mark, or far from it. Whatever the specifics of the years to come, it is clear that everyone will be bombarded with more information faster, faster and faster.

In the short run, the wider availability of computers, fax machines and electronic mail provides new paths for sampling public opinion and for getting news out to the public. The tremendous growth of the Internet in the past few years points the way for the Information Superhighway that was the technology centerpiece of the early Clinton administration.

Whatever the technologies for gathering and delivering information, the opinion triangle will exist in the future as it does today.

The instant reporting of everything, public opinion included, only increases the importance of the relationship between public opinion and the news media. For in times of instant communication, the media are the only available source of information. It just takes too much time to see what your coworkers or friends or relatives think; you need to make up your mind now.

Such a world of instant information is fraught with danger. Under such time pressure, it will be extremely difficult for journalists to make informed judgments about what is important and what is not, about what is truthful and what is not. This means that even more unfiltered information will be available to the public. Today's CNN may seem very slow by comparison.

The demands for instant information and instant analysis will push the journalist to make quicker and quicker decisions. Some of these will be supported by better and faster information technology that will provide more information faster than ever. With increasing use of intelligent analysis systems, the journalist will be less burdened with useless information.

But in a world like that, understanding of the pitfalls of public opinion surveys and other precision journalism will be even more important.

That faster, smaller world needs to be summarized more carefully and more completely. Techniques such as those discussed in this book will become more and more central to journalism in the years to come. The premium will be on analysis techniques, finding the gems of information in the piles of rocks, and finding them faster and understanding them faster and reporting them faster.

A FINAL WORD

As you have read this book, we hope that you have come to understand in some depth how public opinion, polls and journalism are intertwined. It has been our goal to provide the tools you as a journalist—or as an informed citizen—need to discriminate between the reliable surveys of public opinion and the junk. In addition, we have sought to describe the analytical methods that can be used to discern the important results in a poll and to place those results in a meaningful historical context. And finally, we have tried to provide a guide for journalists to turn those meaningful poll results into an interesting and accurate story.

The growing links between journalism, polls and public opinion place ever heavier burdens on those who conduct, analyze and report public opinion polls. The task is getting harder, and it must be completed faster and faster.

Welcome to the future.

Appendix A

THE WORLD'S SHORTEST COURSE IN STATISTICS

In order to understand much of what occurs in the world around us, we need to understand some things about statistics. For a journalist, this knowledge is even more important because he or she needs to determine what is newsworthy, what should be included in a story.

The term "statistic" refers to numerical facts, numbers that describe or summarize information. The study of statistics includes a wide variety of different types of numerical facts. For the purposes of this quick course, we will concentrate on the statistical knowledge needed to evaluate public opinion polls.

First, we will discuss the concept of statistical significance. Second, we will talk about samples and sampling. Finally, we will take a look at the issue of causality, which is often a stumbling block in the presentation of stories on public opinion.

STATISTICAL SIGNIFICANCE

In the analysis of information, one of the most difficult questions is whether the observed phenomenon is real or due solely to chance. This type of analysis comes to us instinctively. If all events in life were random, we would have a pretty difficult time learning what to do. On the other hand, while the real world contains many things that seem to be random, we find many others that we can learn to anticipate and therefore behave appropriately.

The problem arises when we need to determine if a specific event is or is not random, that is, occurring as a result of chance or luck. Let us begin with a simple example. Take a coin and flip it. If it comes up heads, would you conclude that this coin is a special coin, that it always comes up heads when you flip it? If the evidence of a single flip is sufficient to bring you to that conclusion, there are a number of people in New York City who would like to talk with you about buying a bridge across the East River.

In fact, you have learned that a single flip of the coin is not adequate evidence. What about two flips? Three? If you flipped the coin four times and it came up heads each time, would you be willing to bet that this is a special coin? In order to determine whether it is likely that such an event could occur, purely by chance, you need to understand some things about probability.

Let us examine another example of this problem. A professor of psychology calls your newspaper to tell you of a wonderful new discovery. He has found a special group of white rats that are right-footed. He tells you that this potential breakthrough in animal behavior has important consequences for genetic analysis. When you visit him in his laboratory, he demonstrates his research by putting five of his special white rats, randomly selected from a group of white rats, into a maze. All of them turn right at the first junction. None turn left. Based upon this demonstration, he expects you to write a story about his research.

How does one know whether an event such as this occurred because of chance or luck? It is impossible to know with certainty. However, one can calculate the probability that this result occurred purely by chance.

For example, on any given flip of a fair, unbiased coin, the chance of its landing heads up is 50 percent, or one in two. Since we are pretty sure that coins don't have any memory, each flip of the coin is independent of every other flip. We pick up the coin again, put it into our hand and flip it. The results of the first flip have *no* impact on the results of the second flip, so the chance of it landing heads up on the second flip is 50 percent, or one in two.

This is a tough concept for many people to understand. When they look at two flips of the coin, they view the flips as connected.

If you ask people "What is the most likely result of flipping a coin the fifth time after it has come up heads four times in a row?," you will likely get two kinds of answers. The first group of people will tell you that it is very unlikely that the coin will come up heads again, since it has already "beat the odds" and come up heads four times in a row. The second group will tell you that it will likely come up heads because it has already shown that heads is more likely than tails.

In fact, if the coin is unbiased, the probability of heads on that fifth flip is, yes, 50 percent, or one in two. The coin doesn't know what the last four flips were, so the chances are the same.

But is the coin biased, more likely to come up one way or another? One can calculate the probability of four heads in a row with an unbiased coin. Since each flip has a 50 percent chance of coming up heads, one can multiply the chances to find the final probability. In this case, 50 percent times 50 percent times 50 percent times 50 percent equals 6.25 percent. So the likelihood that this result would occur is a little more than six times in every 100 experiments of four coin tosses. Would you conclude that this coin is biased?

That would depend upon what was at stake. Would you be willing to bet a quarter on the next flip? What about betting $100? Would you bet your life? I don't think so. If the coin is not biased, the chances are 50 percent that you would lose.

What if the coin has been flipped six times? What about seven? At what point do you become quite sure that the coin is biased? That really depends upon how important the results are. If we are talking about betting a small amount of money, you might well be satisfied with a 60 percent chance of being correct. If you are betting your life, you might want odds of 1 million to 1 or better.

This "level of confidence" in the results is often overlooked in reporting statistical information. Most often, the level of confidence discussed is 95 percent, that is, the probability of getting results like these purely from chance is less than 5 percent.

If you flip a coin five times, and it comes up heads all five times, then the probability of this happening with an unbiased coin is a little more than three in 100.

But wait a minute. What about the coin coming up tails on each of five tosses? This has the same probability as five heads. So the potential for a coin's coming up with five straight flips in one result or five straight flips in the other is twice the probability, or more than six in 100. This is because the probability of getting five heads in a row is a little more than 3 percent and the probability of getting five tails in a row is a little more than 3 percent. These are both possible outcomes of the experiment; therefore we can add them together to determine what the chances are of getting either one outcome or the other.

To be sure we have an unbiased coin, we have to consider both types of extreme results. So we really need to have six flips in a row of the same result to be more than 95 percent confident that this coin is truly biased, that our results were not just due to chance. The actual probability of getting either six heads in a row or six tails in a row is .03125, less than 5 percent.

So far we have looked at two important concepts: how sure you need to be and how you tell whether something is beyond that level of significance. How sure you need to be depends upon what you will do with the results. You tell whether something is significant by calculating the probability of getting that type of result, or one equally or even more extreme, purely due to chance.

Now let us return to our favorite rats in the maze. What is the probability of a rat's turning right rather than left? We really don't know. Maybe all rats are right-footed and turn right all the time. We can test this hypothesis by running a group of rats through the maze. If right and left are equally likely, what is the probability of six rats in a row all turning right or all turning left? The same as a coin flip, .03125 (.5 x .5 x .5 x .5 x .5 x .5). So we can test to see if these rats behave randomly or not.

Please note that in order for this experiment to work correctly, neither the rats nor the maze can have a memory of what happened before. If you ran the rats once before and fed them in the right branch of the maze, they would no longer behave randomly even if their behavior was random to begin with. You certainly would not want to run the same rat over and over again. Rats do have memory.

But we have to remember that the psychology professor has told us that white rats are special, they are different from other rats. Since we don't know exactly what rats are like, and since we don't have any way to measure all rats or even all white rats, we are going to have to find a way to take a smaller number of rats to represent the entire population of rats. This subset is called a sample.

The process of taking a sample is covered below. Here, the important thing is that we have a sample of two kinds of rats: special white rats and regular rats. The professor has concluded that the two types of rats are different. Before we write a story, we want to be quite certain, say 95 percent certain, of the results. We will still report them as statistical results significant at the 95 percent confidence level, because there would still be a 5 percent chance that the results occurred by luck. We don't ever want to write a story that goes beyond the confidence that the statistics give us in the experiment.

First, we need to know how regular rats perform in the maze. If rats have a 50 percent chance of turning right or left (sometimes called nonsystematic or random behavior), what would we expect the results to be if we run ten rats through the maze? We would expect five to turn left and five to turn right. When you take a class in probability and statistics, you will learn that while this is the most likely outcome, there are a variety of other reasonably probable outcomes like six right and four left, or four right and six left.

This is not different from a series of coin flips. If you flip ten coins, you will most likely get five heads and five tails, but other results are also reasonably likely. The more trials attempted, the more likely that the results, if the coins are unbiased or the rats turn left and right by chance, will come close to 50 percent each outcome.

Why this is the case should be intuitively obvious. If you have a bag of 500 green and 500 red marbles, mix them thoroughly and then pick ten marbles, a single extra red marble makes a big difference in the outcome. If you pick 100, then one makes much less of a difference. There are specific mathematical rules that govern the impact of increasing the sample size on the variability of the sample results. These will become very important to us as we look at sample sizes.

Let us return to the rats in a maze. To be helpful in our mathematics, we will assume that we know that regular rats exhibit nonsystematic or random behavior in turning right and left in a maze. On the basis of that knowledge, we will conclude that the behavior of rats in the general population is random in terms of left and right turns in the maze; each outcome is equally likely.

We now test our white rats. Of the first ten rats, nine turn right and one turns left. What do we conclude?

This result is a little more difficult to calculate because we have to find the probability of any result this extreme or more extreme.

The first question we need to answer is whether we have to consider the chances that the white rats are really left-footed. Since our hypothesis for testing is that these rats are right-footed, we are not concerned about the chance that they might turn left purely by luck. So our only concern is whether they might be turning right purely by chance. We therefore have to calculate the probability that as many or even more rats would turn right purely by chance. If rats are nonsystematic, then the chance of turning left and right is equal, 50 percent. We also know that there are 1,024 possible results of this experiment, ranging from all left turns to all right turns. This is calculated by taking the number of possible results of a single trial and raising it to the power of the number of trials, that is, 2^{10}, which is 1,024. Of these 1,024 cases, there is exactly one where all rats turned right. There are ten cases where nine turned right and one turned left. Thus, there are only 11 results out of 1,024 that are as extreme or more extreme than what we got. The probability of getting the result nine turning right and one turning left, or a more extreme result in the same direction, is 11/1024, or 1.1 percent. We would conclude from this result that these rats are not random in their behavior, that they are right turners to some degree.

If the results were eight turning right and two turning left, the number of cases out of 1,024 that are that extreme or more so would be 56. These 56 cases include the one case where all turn right; 10 cases of nine turning right and one turning left; and 45 cases of eight turning right and two turning left. This leads to a probability of 56/1024, which is 5.47 percent. Even though this seems like a very unlikely outcome, we are unable to conclude, with 95 percent confidence, that these rats are right-footed; and they might be nonsystematic.

The larger the number of rats run through the maze, the smaller the difference that is required to be significant. In the last example, 80 percent of the rats went right, but it was not significant at the 95 percent level. If you ran fifteen rats—50 percent more— through the maze, and 80 percent still turned right (twelve out of fifteen), the probability would be 576 results out of 32,768 possible outcomes, or 2.0 percent. This is a result that is clearly significant at the 95 percent level of confidence.

The more results in the experiment, the greater the confidence in the same distribution of results. This applies directly to the analysis of public opinion polls.

So far we have covered three important topics. The first was the level of significance required. This depends upon what you will use the information for. The second is whether the result is significant at that level. We had to calculate the probability of getting a result as extreme or more extreme purely by chance. We also had to decide what direction of results to consider—both right and left turns, for example. We also touched on the use of a sample and on the impact of sample size on our confidence in the results.

SAMPLES AND SAMPLING

Everyone is familiar with samples; we use them every day. A sample is nothing more than a part of something taken to show what the rest is like. At a smorgasbord, we may sample many foods to decide which ones we want to take full portions of. Our doctor may take a sample of blood to see how we are doing. An electronics company may test a sample of its products to ensure quality. In each of these cases, a subset of a larger group has been selected.

All of these are samples, and all are useful. Many people seem to feel that taking a sample is not quite right, that using the entire universe is a much better idea. Certainly there are times when such a process, called a census in public opinion terms, is preferable. But when you visit the doctor, you don't want him to test all of your blood, even if it would improve the accuracy of the test significantly.

In order to understand samples, the first step is to understand what the overall group to be studied is, the universe. This can vary from study to study. For example, if you are interested in voting behavior, it is not likely that you will want to talk with children between two and twelve years of age. On the other hand, if you want to understand viewing of cartoons on Saturday mornings, adults over eighteen would not be the right group. So the first step in taking a sample is to know what the sample is of.

This is a key decision in any project involving sampling: What is the population or universe to be sampled? The results of the sample can be projected only to the universe that is sampled. In our example of white rats above, we would be unable to make any statements about gray rats, since they were not part of the universe to be sampled. Similarly, if you included only people who subscribed to a specific magazine in your universe, you would not be able to generalize to the population as a whole.

The choice of a universe is critically important to any sampling project. The definition of the target universe should come from the design of the study, not after the fact, from the sample you were able to get. Very interesting results from surveys of undergraduate political science students at the local university are not very important to questions about politics in your town.

But it is important to examine the population to make sure that the study is possible. For example, if you have to survey via telephone, your sample is only of those who have telephones. In many countries, this is not a very good sample of the entire population. In the United States, it may or may not be, depending upon the nature of the study. If you are trying to study the homeless or the very poor, a universe of all households having telephones would not be a useful one.

Once a reasonable population or universe is defined, the next question is what type and size sample is needed.

There are many different types of samples. The key to the type of sample is that the probability of selection for every element is known. As a result, the statistician can adjust the sample, usually called weighting, for imbalances caused specifically by the sampling methodology. This is not the sampling error that is normally discussed; rather, it is the error introduced because not everyone in the population had an equal probability of being chosen for the sample. In a properly conducted survey, this correction will eliminate this error.

For our purposes, we will only talk about "random" samples even though this type is seldom if ever used in polls. This type is a sample where the probability of selection is equal for each member of the population. Most surveys, once the corrections are applied to the sampling frame, are treated as if they resulted from a random sample.

In a perfect world, you would know important information about the population before you had to design the sample. For example, it would be useful to know how the characteristics you wish to measure are distributed in the population. Let us say that you are interested in measuring the height of the population aged twenty-one through fifty on Oomlaudville Island. If you knew how variable the height was from person to person, you could figure out how many people you would need to measure to ensure your results, at the 95 percent confidence interval, within two inches. The best example of this occurs when there is no variation at all. If everyone who lives on the island is five feet, ten inches tall, how many do you need in your sample to estimate the average height of the population? That's right, a sample of one. The same is true if all belong to one political party, if they have the same opinion of current economic conditions and so on. Only if there is some variation do we have a problem with sample size.

In the real world, we are taking a sample because we don't know what the population looks like. The only clue we have is the results in the sample. The statistician will explain that we estimate the variation in the universe from the variation in the sample. But if we don't know what the estimated variance is in the population until we take the sample, how can we choose the size of the sample? Fortunately, there are some techniques that can help us to choose a sample size for a specific population.

Statisticians have prepared tables of sample sizes required for a specific confidence interval for a specific population size. These tables also take into account how evenly distributed the measured characteristic is. For example, if you were measuring what percentage of the population had blue eyes, your results would be more accurate, in terms of percentages, if the results were very rare, say less than 5 percent of the population. This would mean that it is not very likely that you would get too many people with blue eyes in the sample and it would not be possible to get a result too low by more than 5 percent, since the percentage in the sample cannot be less than zero. For most polls, however, we would choose the worst case, a distribution close to 50 percent.

In this case, given a population of 100,000 in order to have a confidence of 95 percent that the result would be within 5 percent of the sample results, we would need a sample of 384. To be confident that the result would be within 2 percent, we would need a sample of 2,345.

In larger populations—over 500,000—the required number for the 95 percent confidence interval and results of plus or minus 3 percent is 1,065, just about what most public national polls use as a sample.

Note that a significant increase in sample size is required to improve the precision of the sample. For example, with a large population, to move the 95 percent confidence interval from plus or minus 4 percent to plus or minus 2 percent requires a sample size increase from 600 to 2,390, almost four times as many.

Clearly, precision is expensive, since the costs of a survey are mostly related to the sample size.

We have learned that we need to define the universe in order to have a sample; that we need to determine the precision we require; that we can determine from those two items what size sample is needed.

Chapter 8 details how samples may be chosen for polls.

CAUSALITY, A POTENTIAL TRAP FOR JOURNALISTS

One of the key problems in reporting information gathered from surveys and other forms of precision journalism is a tendency to come to conclusions that are not justified by the data. The most difficult problem area is the difference between association and causality.

Perhaps an illustration can help. The rooster crows every morning and then the sun comes up. If the rooster believes that his crowing causes the sun to rise, he has made a serious error; he has mistaken association for cause.

Social science brings us another famous example. A study of Scandinavian cities showed that the number of storks observed in the cities was associated with the number of births in the cities. Those cities with a large number of storks had a large number of births, and those with a small number of storks had a small number of births. The statistic which measures that association is usually a correlation. In this case, the statistic was not only significant, beyond the 95 percent confidence interval, it was a very powerful association. Would you conclude that there is a causal relationship between storks and births? In fact, the real relationship is between the population size of the city and the two measured items. The more people, the more births. The more people, the more houses, and therefore the greater the number of places for storks to roost. Therefore, the greater the number of people, the greater the number of storks and of births.

What is most important for the journalist to recognize is that it is very unlikely that any survey can provide true evidence of "cause." Association can be measured and reported, but cause is difficult. Even if we know that those who eat red meat have a higher-than-average risk of heart attack, that information is not enough to prove that it is red meat that "causes" a heart attack. It might be that type A people are more likely to eat red meat, or some other associated measure might be the true "cause" of the heart attack.

In order to measure causality, researchers normally need to conduct experiments where other variables can be controlled and where the value of the associations can be truly tested.

Journalists should be extremely careful of any claims of causality. Most important, any story about associations must be carefully worded not to imply causality.

TWENTY QUESTIONS

This appendix is a summary of the questions included in the pamphlet written by the authors and published by the National Council on Public Polls. Copies of the pamphlet can be obtained by contacting the NCPP office at 800-239-0909.

1. Who did the poll?
2. Who paid for the poll and why was it done?
3. How many people were interviewed for the survey?
4. How were those people chosen?
5. What area—nation, state or region—or what group—teachers, lawyers, Democratic voters, etc.—were these people chosen from?
6. Are the results based on the answers of all the people interviewed?
7. Who should have been interviewed and was not?
8. When was the poll done?
9. How were the interviews conducted?
10. Is this a dial-in poll, a mail-in poll or a subscriber coupon poll?
11. What is the sampling error for the poll results?
12. What other kinds of mistakes can skew poll results?
13. What questions were asked?

14.   In what order were the questions asked?

15.   What other polls have been done on this topic? Do they say the same thing? If they are different, why are they different?

16.   So the poll says the race is all over. What now?

17.   Was the poll part of a fund-raising effort?

18.   So I've asked all the questions. The answers sound good. The poll is correct, right?

19.   With all these potential problems, should we ever report poll results?

20.   Is this poll worth reporting?

An additional source for journalists is the American Association for Public Opinion Research (AAPOR). They can be reached at 313-764-1555.

BIBLIOGRAPHY

American Enterprise Institute. 1993. Seminar on Political Polling. Washington, D.C. December 6.

Biemer, Paul P.; Groves, Robert M.; Lybert, Lars E.; Mathiowetz, Nancy A; and Sudman, Seymour. 1991. *Measurement Errors in Surveys*. New York: John Wiley and Sons.

Bishop, George F.; Oldendick, Robert W.; Tuchfarber, Alfred J.; and Bennett, Stephen E. 1980. "Pseudo-Opinions on Public Affairs." *Public Opinion Quarterly*, 44(2): 189–209.

Bishop, George, and Smith, Andrew. 1993. "Response-Order Experiments in the Gallup Poll: Effects and Explanations." Paper presented at the AAPOR Conference, Batavia, Illinois, May.

Brace, Paul, and Hinckley, Barbara. 1992. *Follow the Leader: Opinion Polls and the Modern Presidents*. New York: Basic Books.

Bradburn, Norman M., and Sudman, Seymour. 1988. *Polls and Surveys*. New York: Jossey-Bass.

Cantril, Albert H. 1980. *Polling on the Issues*. Cabin John, Md.: Seven Locks Press.

Converse, Jean M. 1987. *Survey Research in the United States: Roots and Emergence, 1890–1960*. Berkeley: University of California Press.

Editor and Publisher. 1981. "CBS Errs in New Jersey." November 28:27.

Fenby, Jonathan. 1986. *The International News Services*. New York: Schocken Books.

Fowler, Floyd J., Jr. 1993. *Survey Research Methods, Second Edition*. Newbury Park, Calif.: Sage.

Gans, Herbert J. 1980. *Deciding What's News: A Study of CBS Evening News, NBC Nightly News, Newsweek and Time.* New York: Vintage Books.

Groves, Robert M. 1989. *Survey Errors and Survey Costs.* New York: John Wiley and Sons.

Groves, Robert M.; Biemer, Paul P.; Lybert, Lars E.; Massey, James T.; Nicholls, William L., II; and Waksbert, Joseph. 1988. *Telephone Survey Methodology.* New York: John Wiley and Sons.

Kagay, Michael. 1993. "For the Poll Watcher, How to Sift Results." *New York Times.* October 17.

Krosnik, Jon A. 1989. "Question Wording and Reports of Survey Results." *Public Opinion Quarterly* 53(1): 106.

Lavrakas, Paul J., and Holley, Jack K., eds. 1991. *Polling and Presidential Election Coverage.* Newbury Park, Calif.: Sage.

Levy, Paul S., and Lemeshow, Stanley. 1991. *Sampling of Populations: Methods and Applications.* New York: John Wiley and Sons.

Mann, Thomas E., and Orren, Gary R., eds. 1992. *Media Polls in American Politics.* Washington, D.C.: Brookings Institution.

Markel, Lester. 1972. *What You Don't Know Can Hurt You.* New York: Quadrangle Books.

McIntyre, Bryce T. 1991. *Advanced Newsgathering.* Westport, Conn.: Praeger.

Meyer, Philip. 1991. *The New Precision Journalism.* Bloomington: Indiana University Press.

Mitofsky, Warren J., and Edelman, Murray. 1993. "A Review of the 1992 VRS Exit polls." Paper presented at the 1993 meeting of the American Association for Public Opinion Research, St. Charles, Ill.

Moore, David. 1992. *The Super Pollsters.* New York: Four Walls Eight Windows.

Robinson, John P., and Meadow, Robert. 1982. *Polls Apart.* Cabin John, Md.: Seven Locks Press.

Roll, Charles W., and Cantril, Albert H. 1972. *Polls: Their Use and Misuse in Politics.* Cabin John, Md.: Seven Locks Press.

Rosenstiel, Tom. 1993. *Strange Bedfellows: How Television and the Presidential Candidates Changed American Politics.* New York: Hyperion.

Rothenberg, Stuart. 1983. *The Political Report* 6(15): 11.

Sheatsley, Paul B., and Mitofsky, Warren J. 1992. *A Meeting Place.* Ann Arbor, Mich.: AAPOR.

Shuman, Howard, and Presser, Stanley. 1981. *Questions and Answers in Attitude Surveys.* New York: Academic Press.

Stephens, Michael. 1988. *A History of News: From the Drum to the Satellite.* New York: Viking.

Sudman, Seymour. 1976. *Applied Sampling.* New York: Academic Press.

Tufte, Edward R. 1983. *The Visual Display of Quantitative Information.* Cheshire, Conn.: Graphics Press.

_____. 1990. *Envisioning Information.* Cheshire, Conn.: Graphics Press.

Weiss, Anne E. 1979. *Polls and Surveys: A Look at Public Opinion Research.* New York: Franklin Watts.

Wilhoit, G. Cleveland, and Weaver, David H. 1980. *Newsroom Guide to Polls and Surveys.* Washington, D.C.: American Newspaper Publishers Association.

Young, Michael. 1992. *Dictionary of Polling.* Westport, Conn.: Greenwood Press.

INDEX

About the Authors

SHELDON R. GAWISER is president of Gawiser Associates, Inc., of Fairfield, Connecticut, consultants in information collection and management. He is senior poll analyst for NBC News and president of the National Council on Public Polls.

G. EVANS WITT is assistant bureau chief of The Associated Press in Washington, D.C. Previously he served as director of AP/NBC News polling.